301.44
HOE

25323

Hoenig, Gary

Reaper

Lodi High   4.31

DATE DUE

Reaper

The Story of a Gang Leader

by GARY HOENIG

The Bobbs-Merrill Company, Inc.

Indianapolis/New York

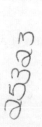

Completed in trust and love
with Barbara;
for Jessica and The Twelfth
Street Hoenigs

If anything seems even more imposing and impossible than writing a book, it is acknowledging all those who helped make it possible. With that in mind, here is a brief list of those who lent me their strength, their intelligence, and, above all, their love, while I stumbled to the finish:

Georgie and the Morton Place Reapers, who are real people, and without whom there would be no book.

Frank Lima of SERA, whose street contacts were invaluable.

Johnson Stevens, for research and assorted other duties that gave him a royal pain in the ass.

Sociologist Goldie Satt, for help of all kinds, and, most of all, for her friendship.

Sociologist Jan Zyniewski, likewise.

Drs. Devra Davis, Betty Weidman, and Frank Warner, whose criticism of earlier drafts was most helpful.

Robert Stock, Al Marlens, and John Van Doorn, for teaching me more about writing and reporting than I can ever hope to absorb.

Harriet Heyman, for a tough and tireless pencil.

Phillip Spitzer, for unfailing moral support.

And to all the others who had to live with me while I struggled through this past year.

Thanks.

GARY HOENIG
October, 1974

II

Georgie was only nine when he moved to the Bronx. He moved there from 118th Street and Lexington Avenue with two brothers and two baby sisters, his mother, and his grandmother. His father had left them six months before. That's when his mother started drinking a lot. Then his grandmother asked them to move in with her, in a new apartment in the Bronx.

Not that his parents were so bad. He was the youngest until he was five, and he was everybody's baby. His looks favored his mother, light skin and dark features, except for his hair, which grew like a sculpted piece of reddish black steel wool in perfect rows around his head. Both his parents loved him, but the two of them were like separate families, each close to him in a deliberately private way. They hardly spoke to each other, because they had little to say to each other. His mother prayed in Spanish each night before going to bed; his father never prayed at all and was constantly correcting her English. Except for trips to the market she hardly went anywhere. Her family was her life, though not out of choice. His father slept during the day and was gone during the night. When he had a job he would sleep on the weekends and be gone for twenty-four hours at a time.

Somehow the whole thing worked. His parents had a kind of unspoken agreement, like two old enemies beyond hate but not beyond pride. She would say nothing about his night life; he would let her run the house the way she wanted. He spent most of his nights at the corner bar, drinking beers that grew flatter as the evening wore on, watching the faded picture on the TV set in the corner. Or, during endless summers, shooting pool and playing cards. When the night began to lift away, he would walk home and would sleep on the sofa. When Georgie got up in the morning, his sprawled, sleeping father was the first thing he saw.

One morning, when he was eight, he got up and there was no one on the sofa. And, that afternoon, he came home to find his mother in the hall, screaming in Spanish, a butcher knife in her hand. Melendez, the super, and another guy who lived in the building held her by the arms. Across from them was another cluster of three; Mrs. Nuñez, their neighbor, was also screaming, and she, too, had a knife. Another pair of half-embarrassed, half-terrified men were holding her arms while trying to avoid her flailing heels. His mother was cursing Mrs. Nuñez for stealing her man.

By the next day, Georgie knew his father was not coming home again.

Georgie didn't want to leave East Harlem. From his fire escape, he could see trucks and cars heading downtown on Lexington Avenue, headed for the guts of the city. Thousands of men and women and children, going to work, going shopping, or going nowhere at a hurried pace. The white spray trucks that sometimes came down the street and washed the litter into the sewers, sending up a fine, cold mist that drifted up and touched his cheeks. And there were plenty of kids his age to play with. They played scully and stickball and wrestled and punched one another, and ran after one another between the parked cars and into the street, sometimes brushing against the fender of a moving car and scaring the driver to death.

But that wasn't a problem in the summer; the street was closed to traffic during the day. When the sun went down behind the pink projects on Park Avenue, he and his friends didn't stop playing. They went on tirelessly until, one by one, their mothers would call out their names from the windows which looked down upon the streets. Georgie was one of the last ones in.

Since his father had gone, his mother had become quiet and strange. She spent too much time drinking and would lie on her bed, eyes wide, staring at the ceiling, a bottle of rum or bourbon standing on the floor next to the bed. Once Georgie came quietly into the bedroom to shut off the light, thinking she was asleep. She rolled over suddenly. He saw her eyes—they were yellow and lined with bright red. Frightened, he stepped back quickly and knocked over a half-empty bottle. She looked down at the yellowish river trickling across the floor and started shrieking. He ran out and hid in the stairwell, remaining there, asleep, until his brother woke him and carried him inside to bed.

On a muggy August morning, they stuffed a few pieces of furniture and a dozen cartons of assorted other junk into a U-haul and moved in with his grandmother. The apartment was much roomier than the old one. Georgie got to share a room with his older brother, instead of being cramped in with all four of the other children. His grandmother didn't speak English too well, and she was always yelling at him for some little thing. But it felt good to know that she would have a hot meal on the table once a day and fresh sheets on the bed every once in a while. Even so, Georgie was very unhappy in this strange place: he had no friends here, and the new school year was only a couple of weeks away.

In East Harlem, he had school pretty much figured out. He started playing hooky when he was seven. He found it impossible to sit on the hard wooden seats for six hours a day and listen to the teacher whine on about things that seemed so foreign to his life. Teachers were always making a big deal about little things, like talking in the lunchroom or playing around in the hall. The worst part was when he sat with his head on the desk, nearly asleep, and the teacher would scream in his ear and give him a shove. He rarely got into real trouble, though, since he was quiet and generally kept to himself. The good days were when they just left Georgie alone, and he was happy that most days were like that.

The teachers, he found, were preoccupied with the kids who made all the noise. He discovered that, if he was quiet and quick, he could slip out of the building in the afternoon and do what he wanted. Soon Georgie got the idea of just not going at all. Nobody seemed to notice. He didn't know whether his mother knew or not, but she never said anything. She never asked him about school, anyway. His father, when he was with them, used to ask Georgie about it all the time, though he never listened for an answer.

Now he would be going to a new school, in the Bronx, and he was afraid—afraid he would have to spend all those hours locked up in there, with no way to sneak out and nothing to do if he did. The last couple of months he lived in Harlem, he did pretty much as he pleased, since his mother was in bed so much of the time. But now that they were living with his grandmother, he had to let her know where he was going whenever he went out. He was sure that it would be much harder to stay out of school with her around. Sure enough, when the first day came, she laid out his clothes and marched him to school herself. It was all he could do to keep from running away from her right there in front of the school. If there was one thing the old lady wanted, it was for Georgie to get an education.

But the other children were on his grandmother's mind as well, and the false warmth of October had not yet subsided when he skipped his first day at the new school. If anything, it was easier than it had been downtown. In East Harlem, his class was almost all Puerto Rican, and even the tough pudgy middle-aged Jewish women teachers spoke a smattering of Spanish. In the Bronx school, the students were a crazy quilt of black and Puerto Rican kids, and a few white children whose parents could never quite afford to move away. The halls and stairways were seething with bodies, pushing, punching, kicking, and running. And the teachers were almost as crazy. Once he had sat and watched in silence, incredulous and afraid, as a 250-pound woman chased two eight-year-old black kids round and round a twenty-foot-square classroom for forty-five minutes. It was so easy to get up and walk out that he couldn't understand why there were any kids left in the school by three o'clock.

Once out on the street, Georgie began to survey the neighborhood. He lived between 182nd and 183rd Streets, in the Fordham section. From his window at night he could hear the distant pounding of the Jerome Avenue el. The street was lined with five- and six-story apartment buildings, white brick turned yellow, or red brick streaked with black. They were crushed together in a valley between the el to the north and the Grand Concourse, which ran on a slightly elevated course two blocks to the south. The big cross streets, 183rd Street and East Burnside Avenue, were littered with dirty stores and fast food stops. The two big avenues twisted through the hard Bronx bedrock, then plunged into tunnels that ran underneath the Concourse, separating the tenements from the luxury buildings and landscaped dividers up above.

After a month of on-and-off hooky playing, Georgie figured he knew the day side of his neighborhood. He knew that at about nine o'clock, the bus on Burnside was crowded enough so he could slip in the back door or climb through a window and catch a ride over to Crotona Park. He knew that the corner grocer on 182nd Street used to leave a couple of ripe melons on the sidewalk on cold mornings; Georgie would take them and have chilled melon for lunch. He knew which of the dozen or so big dogs on the block were really vicious, and not just mean looking. He knew the alleys and driveways, the fences and basements, the sharp concrete-and-wire topography of the neighborhood; if he wanted to, he could slip away unnoticed on one street and not come back into view until he was three or four blocks away. He was a roof hurdler, a fence climber, a pavement gymnast.

His first friends there were three kids who lived on the block: Steam, a tall, thin boy with big horn rims that made his eyes look like they were popping out; Jackie, who was older and bigger than the others, with a leonine face and a mean streak that helped him push the others around; and Dink, an undersized peanut of a kid who was perfect for begging quarters in the park.

By early spring, the four had a steady thing going. When the weather was good, they would meet at about nine in front of the pizzaria on 183rd Street and grab a free bus ride over to the park. Jackie had a beat-up basketball that his brother had given him, and they would try shooting baskets for a while, dribbling intensely and then desperately flinging the heavy ball at the basket, hoping that the ball might somehow reach the rim and roll in. When they tired of that, they would walk through the park and throw rocks at the birds and the squirrels. Or they would walk from Crotona park to the Bronx zoo, carefully imitating the cool strutting march of the older boys on the block. They would cross streets in the middle of heavy traffic and bang on the fenders of moving cars as they went by. They liked to make fun of the old people in the park, who wore their fright like gray masks and made great targets. Sometimes they would run into groups of kids visiting the zoo on a school trip, and that would be the most fun of all. They would dart in and out of the neat double line, grabbing little purses and school bags, pushing bodies left and right, and then howling with laughter while the nervous teacher desperately tried to control the group.

Then there was the run-in with the zoo guard. It happened on what started out as a pretty ordinary day, except that nobody but Dink and Georgie showed up at the pizza joint. They waited for a while, and then just started walking east down Burnside, hoping to run into somebody else. By noon they had walked to and all through the zoo, past the lion island, and into the zoo cafeteria, where they stopped for a break.

Georgie bought a bag of potato chips. They sat near the entrance, watching the meager weekday crowd pass by. Soon, a black guy in a blue security uniform walked past the empty tables, bought a cup of coffee and a shapeless piece of pastry, and sat down a few tables away. The only sound in the place was the gentle swishing of a mop; someone was listlessly cleaning the floor behind them.

They watched the uniformed man chew purposefully on the dough.

"Looks like he's chewing shit, don't he?" said Dink, and he cracked up. Georgie spat out a mouthful of potato chips and tried hopelessly to fight back the giggles. The security guard shot an angry look at them. Instantly, they shut up tight. They tried not to look at him, but they knew he was glaring at them. The guy started walking over, his shoes clicking on the hard floor.

"What the hell you kids think is so funny?" he said. "And what you doin' here now, anyway? Y'all ought to be in school."

Georgie froze momentarily and looked over at Dink. Suddenly, both jumped up and started running, Dink going out one way, Georgie another. But Georgie ran smack into the floor cleaner and sent pail, mop, himself and the cop sprawling on the wet floor. He scurried to his feet and made a dash. The cop, darting after him, wasn't so lucky. Georgie heard a crash as he ran out, and he resisted the impulse to turn around and laugh.

As he ran past the gate into the zoo, an arm suddenly reached out and spun him around; then he was lifted off the ground and deposited inside a booth where admission was collected. He was trapped, he thought, and his grandmother would kill him. His captor turned to say something to him, but then another body flashed by. The zoo guard spun around and raced after him. Georgie peered out from the booth and watched as the kid turned to face the guard. There was a pause, as the two stared at each other. For a second, Georgie stood paralyzed, fascinated. Then he realized that he could just run out the gate and get away. He turned and saw three other kids waiting in the bushes beyond the turnstiles, motioning him to run out. He bolted out the door and leaped into the bushes. When he turned to see what had happened behind him, he saw the kid run right at the bigger man, juke with his left shoulder, and then cut underneath an outstretched arm and through the gate. The four of them then began to run, dodging cars as they dashed across Southern Boulevard. Then they all jumped on the back bumper of a green city bus. Six or seven blocks later, they casually dropped to the ground and trotted to the sidewalk. Only George bothered to look back.

They turned down a side street, Georgie following, but not too quickly. They stopped on a narrow street that was fenced in, like most others, by dirty gray and red buildings, and leaned against an old Chevy. They sat there gravely, trying not to breathe hard, although beads of sweat sat fatly gleaming on their foreheads. After what seemed to Georgie a very long silence, the kid who had decoyed the guard at the zoo told one of the others to go around the corner and get them some soda. He came back with four stocky bottles of Mission orange soda, and they all leaned back against the car and sucked on the sickly sweet soda.

"What they call you, man?" somebody finally said to Georgie. He looked back at him and blinked. Georgie, he knew, sounded like a little boy's name. "Gee," he finally muttered. "Just Gee."

There was another silence. Georgie was looking at the kid who had saved his ass at the zoo, sizing him up. Noticing that, the kid spoke. "Well, Gee-boy," he said, "if you gonna run with us, you best know who we are. I'm J.J. That's my brothers, Robert and James. The big dude is Mellow." Mellow was already five feet tall. The others looked pretty much alike, except that J.J. was obviously the oldest. Georgie nodded as the others murmured "How you doin'," and "What's happening."

Georgie kept on looking at J.J. He stood there cleaning his nails with a penknife. Though he was no more than a year older than Georgie, he made Georgie feel like a little kid. His face was expressionless. When he smiled, only the corners of his mouth turned up slightly. There was nothing clumsy about the way he moved, and no wasted motion. Georgie was afraid that the first thing he would say would make him look foolish in J.J.'s eyes, so he said nothing. His only comfort was that none of the others said anything, either. He became aware that they, too, looked to J.J. for approval.

Somebody said, "Let's take him to the hole," and they started walking down the street. After walking for a couple of blocks, they came to a corner where a number of buildings had been condemned to the wrecker's ball. One of the buildings looked as if it were sagging. Right at the corner, below ground level, had been a store of some kind, but there was nothing there now except piles of broken glass and concrete, and twisted, rusting metal. They turned the corner, and J.J. led them into the hallway of the building.

There was very little light, and Georgie could see dark shapes all over the floor. When one of the shapes suddenly moved and scurried away into the blackness, Georgie almost turned and ran out. He had seen many rats before, but he never quite got over being frightened and sick at the sight of them. But the others moved on without noticing, picking their way with ease through the debris, until they came to a staircase and started climbing. They went up two flights, and then turned down the hall. Georgie could see that a few people had once lived here, because the hallway still resembled that of an apartment building, and the doors that remained still had the names of the families that lived there inset in a little notch above the peephole. As they moved farther along, he was surprised to see that a few people were still living there. Inside a couple of open doorways there were mattresses and boxes of clothing, even a few ashcans which had been used to make fires in. He shivered, thinking how cold it would be to live in the place during the winter.

They came to an apartment that still had a door, only there was a large hole where the lock should have been. By now, Georgie was getting sick of the piss smell that was everywhere. He coughed when he walked into the apartment, because the smell was worse here. There were two rooms in the apartment, but little was left of the rotting partition between them. All the broken glass and empty cans and bottles had been swept into one corner; here the sun came streaming in haphazardly through the shards of the broken window pane. It shined on a newly whitewashed wall, on which was painted, in red spray paint, with elaborate swirls, seven names: Streak, Mellow, Augie, Snoopy, Robo, Jolt, and J.J.

"You put your name up there, Gee-boy," J.J. said. "I'll get you the paint. But first we got a little something you got to do to get behind us." J.J. walked around the partition, disappearing for a second. He returned with a large paper cup, the kind they used for mixing milk shakes at an ice cream stand. J.J. handed the cup to Georgie.

"You take that cup and you piss in it, boy. You piss in it until it's all full up. Then you drink it down. And when you do that, nigger, you can run with us."

Georgie stared at the cup. He looked up at J.J., and J.J. looked back with that blank face of his. The others were silent, as they had been all day. He looked down at the cup. It was a good nine inches deep and looked as big as a quart beer bottle. He couldn't imagine filling it up, much less drinking it all. He swallowed hard and sighed, and then unzipped his pants and took out his penis. He took a few steps away from the bright light of the sun. As he stood trying to urinate, he heard muffled laughter behind him. He turned his head carefully and saw the four of them howling in laughter. He turned toward them and felt the warm liquid on his hand, then on his pants leg as he jerked his hand away. Frantically, he moved the cup back under the stream. Behind him, the others were laughing so hard that they were collapsed on the floor.

When he finished, Georgie put the cup on the window sill, zipped up his pants, and turned to face them. They were standing now, smiling, but wary of what he might do. He felt on the verge of tears, but, instead of crying, he turned, grabbed the cup, and, in one quick motion, threw it at them. J.J. got the worst of it, catching half of it in the face. Georgie started for the door, but James grabbed his legs and sent him headlong into the paperboard partition. Robert grabbed the cup and poured the remainder on Georgie's face. Georgie tackled him, and the two of them rolled around the floor, punching and kicking. Georgie was sure they would kill him now. They would leave him tied up in the building to starve to death and be eaten by the rats. Or they would just pitch him right out the window. He rolled Robert over once more and came out on top, swinging his arms wildly. Robert had his hands up to protect his face, and as he looked through the writhing fingers, Georgie could see that he was still laughing. He hesitated and looked around. The others were standing there watching, smiles on all their faces. He looked back down at Robert. Then he, too, began to smile.

J.J. picked out a bottle of Ripple wine from underneath a broken floorboard. They sat down, ready for a celebration. Robert showed Georgie how to write his name on the white wall with the red spray paint. It took Georgie a while to get the wrist action

needed for the proper flourish in the letters. Finally
he was ready. Very carefully, he wrote out Gee-boy
on the wall, accenting it with a swirling red line underneath.

It was nearly dark when Georgie came home.
His grandmother was waiting for him at the door.
She was angry, but he hardly heard what she said. He
was making plans, anxiously going over in his mind
how to get to J.J.'s house from his house. He gulped
down his dinner, then slipped out the door and ran
downstairs. He was trying to figure out how he would
be able to get a bottle of wine to give to the others.
He had calculated that this would be the most im-
pressive way to repay them. On his way out, he ran
into Dink.

"Hey, Georgie, where you been?" Dink asked.

"Around, man, you know," Georgie answered
distantly.

"Did they take you down to the station house?"
Dink asked.

"What?" Georgie answered, his thoughts else-
where. Then he remembered. "Oh. No, man, I got
away."

"Hey, how'd you do that?" Dink asked, excited
now.

"I just did, man, you know. I'll tell you some
other time," Georgie snapped. Then he added, softly,
"I gotta go."

He started walking away, and Dink called after
him, "Catch you tomorrow morning, man."

"I won't be there," he answered, not bothering
to turn around. "I got things to do."

Hoe Avenue and Southern Boulevard, the Bronx. Probably the worst street in the city. The police precinct there is called Fort Apache because of the no-man's land that surrounds it. Hoe Avenue is endless blocks of filthy, crumbling tenements, some piled high with people, others empty, with no windows and no doors, still others, piles of rubble serving as playgrounds.

The kids crawl up the crumbling bricks like hungry ants. The bricks crumble some more, and the kids come barreling down. Once in a while, a kid's head gets crushed when he slides the wrong way, and a hundred pounds of mortar falls on top of him. But that makes it all the more fun.

The demolished buildings make good garbage dumps, too. Around mid-morning is everyone's favorite time to come by and dump all the garbage that won't fit into the rusted cans that are scattered like spent artillery shells over the pavement. People who live in buildings adjoining the vacant lots have it much easier. They can just pitch their garbage right out their windows. The stench gets bad, but it's not so bad as it would be if the garbage were still inside. The urine smells inside are bad enough. And the garbage outside keeps most of the rats out there instead of on the stairs.

It's safer to be inside after eleven or so. Not just because of the junkies, but also because of the dog packs that start running the streets, especially in summer, as the crowds begin to thin out. There are usually eight to ten dogs in a pack, most of them medium-size mutts, though there are occasionally a few big ones, such as shepherds and danes. They don't hunt people; not yet, anyway. But they are ferocious scavengers that will tear and trample anything that comes between them and their hunting grounds. The dogs are victims too. Late at night, there are people in the street—dope fiends, winos, stray kids—who are hungry enough to attack the dogs and kill them for food. They realize that the dogs are more vulnerable to attack in the darkness. The dogs can't sleep during the day, either, because the kids harass and maim them, pitching them off rooftops or luring them onto highways.

Landlords on Hoe Avenue are collecting rent checks only from the welfare department. They don't know who lives in the buildings; they don't want to. They wouldn't drive down Hoe Avenue in a Brinks truck. The people don't know who owns the buildings; nor do they care. They don't really live

there, anyway. In summer, they live on the stoops
and the sidewalks, except at night; even then, some
sleep on the cool grillwork of the fire escapes. In
winter, they just wait inside for the weather to get
warm.

The sidewalk is thick in summer. The air is so
wet even the bricks sweat. People are everywhere.
There is glass in the street, mounds of dog leavings,
shoes and mattresses and broken pieces of furniture.
The people are angry and ugly, their faces chiseled
into hostile grimaces. There are card tables on the
sidewalk, where men in bare chests or in spotted T
shirts play dominoes and whist and poker. Eighty-
dollar paychecks go to the winners, razor-blade cuts
to the cheats, home and a screaming woman to the
losers.

At the corners, leaning against the walls and cars
and lampposts, are the young men, tomorrow's card
players. They talk incessantly about women and
highs and yesterday's good times. The talking stops
when someone walks by, or when a car stops at the
corner. They size up all strangers, as if selecting their
prey. They feel in themselves the power to make
someone else afraid. Instinctively they turn it on, to
test that power. An old trick is to break a corner
traffic light and stare at a driver as he sits and waits
for the light to change. He waits and waits, as the
light stays a bleary red; he begins to squirm, a corner
of his eye fixed on fifty other eyes staring back. He
catches an evil grin and a knife sawing away at dirty
fingernails. He looks back, and still the light is red.
They're just kids, he thinks. But why are they staring

at me? Someone spits at the car. In answer the car
jerks forward for a second, then stops short. The light
is still red.

But the game gets boring. Finally someone yells
out that the light is broken. What do they want? the
driver thinks. For God's sake, what did they say? He
manages a soft "Huh?" A street choir of voices yells
back, "THE LIGHT IS BROKEN." That takes another thirty seconds to sink in. Then, relieved, he
drives on.

The feeling of street power, though, never gets
boring. It's like dope, it's easy to get up on, to get
addicted to. Especially when there's nothing else.
Nothing to do, nothing to see, nothing to become. A
blank slate, and no chalk to write with. No education,
no skills, no jobs. Money is either begged or stolen.
Identity must be won brutally, purchased with somebody else's pain. Love must be gulped down violently in huge chunks of flesh torn in ritual sexual
combat. Life is sustained by dominating others.

The young ones start with sadistic acts of violence. A cat is thrown off a roof in a paper bag and
left congealed in the brown paper on a doorstep. An
old lady with a heart condition answers the doorbell,
and a cherry bomb explodes in her face. A mongoloid
eight-year-old is left tied to a tree, naked, with a bag
of his own shit tied to his penis.

Later they compete among themselves, riding
the bumpers of city buses, clutching at the tiny space
between the window and the bus frame, leaning
against the bus as the driver takes his turns faster, as
he tries to pitch his unwanted riders out into the

traffic. Or they run up the stairs to the el train, jump the turnstiles, grab a train and ride between the cars. Then on the roofs. Then below the cars, on the trucks. On Sundays, they might walk single file on top of the third rail, the soles of their feet tingling with awareness of the electric pulse vibrating below them.

All the while, the ranks are thinning. Some are maimed or killed. Some are too frightened to continue the game, or too sensitive. They are the first to find solace in the needle, to hide from the sickly yellow summer sun behind a nodding cloud. Dope brings them together, like bats in a cave, to huddle nervously on rooftops and park benches and mumble about deals and hustles and the big score and an early death.

The others are still busy with their games. They have big toys, now, guns and knives, and they shoot and stab one another over imagined insults and adolescent betrayals, trying to bring meaning to where they are. They experiment with penny-ante holdups and disappointing muggings. Once in a while, the frustration of pushing some old man around for a lousy seven dollars and twenty-five cents gets to be too much, and, enraged, a primed-up finger pulls a trigger and kills somebody. The ultimate game. Even then some of them gain a temporary victory, riding the trains again, holing up at the parks and playgrounds, until the heat lets up and even the local precinct gives up.

And a few just get out.

Georgie loved to walk with J.J. He loved the gliding way he moved, his smooth talking, using his own special kind of street talk, the way he had of never raising his voice, even when friends knew he was angry and ready to explode. Georgie was never afraid of anything when he walked down the street with J.J. He had the feeling that if there were a whole crowd in their way, J.J. would part them and make way for him and Georgie.

And J.J. seemed to like being with him, too. On mornings when Georgie had to go to school, he would sometimes find James or Robert outside when he came out. "J.J. said we'd be going over to Crotona Park, and you wouldn't know where to find us," they would say, and they would all grab a bus and ride over to the park. One time, Georgie caught the measles and was stuck home in bed. Around three-thirty, J.J. and his brothers showed up to see how he was. His grandmother wouldn't let them in, fearing they might catch it, too; but it didn't really matter. Their coming had been enough. He sometimes wondered how J.J. knew so much about his comings and goings. But he never had the courage to ask him.

Georgie's biggest problem was his grandmother. In his second term at school, Georgie missed almost two months in a row, and, even in the Bronx, a nine-year-old can't get away with that. His grandmother got a call from the school, and, bad as her English was, she somehow understood that he hadn't been going to school for a while. For a whole week, she walked him to and from school every day. She stood there glaring until he went inside, and as he turned at the first staircase landing, he could see her through the mesh metal screen on the window, still watching the door. When he came down the same staircase in the afternoon, she was standing in exactly the same place, and he wondered if she had gone home at all.

The weeks after that were worse, in a way. She picked odd mornings to walk him there, and different afternoons to meet him afterward. For practically the rest of the term, he had to stay in school for the whole day. He was afraid to take a chance. It was really painful when the spring came and the weather got warmer. Even then, though, it was easier to keep on going to school from nine to three and then come home afterward. By then, his grandmother would be wrapped up in the soap operas on television, and when he would grab his jacket and head for the door, shouting "Be back later," she rarely bothered to answer back. Georgie was glad when the summer finally came. The first day after school was out, he was up earlier than on school days and out of the house before his grandmother could ask him where he was going.

There were eight members in the clique that hung around with J.J. They called themselves the Clinton Hawks, after the street that J.J. lived on, which ran into Crotona Park. Georgie was the only member of the group who didn't live on or near Clinton Avenue. It was a long walk for Georgie; he was lucky the East Burnside bus ran all the way to Clinton. The other members were J.J., James, Robert, Augie, Streak, Mellow, and Snoopy. All except J.J.'s brothers used nicknames; being J.J.'s brothers, they didn't need nicknames.

Augie was a skinny kid named Frank Hopkins, who got his nickname from the cartoon character, Augie Doggy. Streak was Anthony Brown; he was very little and very fast. Mellow was huge and brooding, but even-tempered. Snoopy was just Snoopy; nobody knew his real name.

On summer mornings, they would all meet in their secret apartment. They would sit on the floor and stare at the cracks in the walls for a while. Then they would argue about what they were going to do that day. Two or three of them would start shouting at each other, and then begin to fight. J.J. would let them wrestle on the floor for a while, and then he would kick one of them in the back until he stopped flailing away. "The park, man, the park. Let's hit the park." And they would stomp down the stairs, scaring the rats back into their holes.

On sunny days, they would go to the park and play basketball. Georgie hated basketball, and basketball hated Georgie. He was terrible at it. For one thing, he never trusted the ball. Whenever he had it, he had to keep his eye on it. Dribbling the ball was a soul-wrenching experience for him, because he had to watch where he was going and keep his eye on the ball at the same time. And his fingers were short and stubby, making it difficult to control the ball to begin with.

The ball comes to Georgie. He dribbles once, then looks around, startled, like a doe that has heard a rustle in the grass. He dribbles again. The ball hits his sneaker and rolls away. He stands there watching it roll, amazed. Somebody picks it up and starts dribbling toward him. He watches, still fascinated, his mind blank. Bounce, bounce, up, in, bounce, bounce. The others now are looking at him.

"Why don't you shoot more, Gee-boy?" J.J. would say after a whole afternoon of watching Georgie play soccer with the basketball. "Or play closer to the hoop, you know, like, go for the bounds. You big and strong enough." J.J. was embarrassed, for Georgie and for himself.

"Yeah, right." What does he mean? Georgie would think. I know what he wants, but I don't know how to do it. And all that night, Georgie would sit and think about how to do better. Shoot more. That's it, shoot more.

Georgie is back on the court. The ball bounces into his hands. Two others step up to him, trying to prevent him from moving toward the basket. Georgie

*snatches the ball and turns violently toward the bas-
ket. He hits one kid with his right elbow, knocking
him over and drawing blood from inside his nose. He
jumps forward on both feet and flings the ball
wildly at the basket. He comes crashing down,
knocking the second kid down. The ball lands with
a high pitched ring against the mesh fence. Everybody laughs, even the kid with the bloody nose, even
Georgie, though only because he can't think of anything else to do. "Damn! He's a butcher out there,"
somebody says, and they all stop playing for a while.*

Georgie almost stopped coming around, he was
so embarrassed. Almost as if he sensed this (or maybe
because he was so much better at it than the other
kids), J.J. started phasing basketball out. Instead, the
Hawks started searching for new worlds to conquer.
They started exploring rooftops. They liked the rooftops, especially during the day, because they couldn't
be seen up there, and nobody could hassle them.
They could travel diagonally across an entire city
block in some places just by climbing over low walls,
or occasionally by leaping over three-foot chasms between buildings.

Rooftops were good for all kinds of games. The
Hawks would buy or steal balloons at the local candy
stores and fill them with water. Then they would pile
a whole bunch of them into a large plastic garbage
bag and sneak out on a roof. At first they just dropped
them anywhere, just to see what would happen. If
the roof was five stories or higher, the balloon would
explode with a flat roar, and the water would splatter
like the columns of dust blown up by a plane-

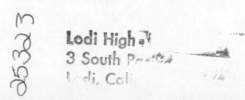

dropped bomb. Fighter pilot: a great game. But more fun with targets. That was the next innovation. People. Big ones, little ones. They learned to be selective. People with bags of groceries in their hands were the best targets. Or old people. Women with baby carriages, or pregnant women, were taboo (but sometimes tempting). Cops, and cop cars, were irresistible. A familiar face, friend or enemy, was bound to meet with a barrage.

The best part was that the victim usually had no idea where the attack came from. Any window from the fourth floor up was a possibility. And even if someone happened to notice one of the Hawks leaning out over the parapet, doing a body count, they could always escape by hopping over a couple of other rooftops and coming down on the other side of the street.

When water balloons got boring, they escalated the war by using bags of dog turds. That, however, proved too dangerous; one victim snuck up the stairs without their knowing and caught them on the roof. He chased them a city block, over the rooftops, and Mellow nearly fell five stories into a mound of garbage when he tripped on the edge of a sheet of hot tar.

Rooftops were also good for being together and being left alone. Little kids, even little kids like J.J., got kicked around a lot on the streets. The seventeen-year-olds kicked the fifteen-year-olds off the basketball court. The fifteen-year-olds did the same to the thirteen-year-olds. So it went, on down the line, with the youngest bearing the brunt of it. The abandoned apartment got too hot in the summer, so the Hawks would stay on the rooftops and pretend it was their turf, instead of their sanctuary.

It was so quiet there, Georgie could barely hear the sounds of the street below. The cars and trucks seemed to murmur their way down the streets; voices seemed distant and higher pitched; and even the clatter of roller skates on the gravelly pavement caught in the wind and hissed gently as it rose to the roof. He could hear the planes before he could see them, growing larger above the bridge to the south. It seemed like hours before they finally roared overhead and passed slowly away to the northwest.

On rainy days, the rooftops were no good at all, especially in the summer, when the rain fell between sheets of lightning that jumped from rooftop to rooftop, hungrily grasping for the largest thing it could find. So the Hawks would go to the movies. They didn't really care what movie was playing, though they liked action movies like *The Dirty Dozen,* or horror movies like *Dracula Returns from the Grave.* But, once there, they hardly spent any time looking at the screen.

Instead, they would take over a whole bank of seats and terrorize everyone in the place. They would grab popcorn boxes from kids walking back to their seats and pour the popcorn all over them and anyone else nearby. They would stand at the soda machines and demand fifteen cents from a kid to buy a soda, then grab the cup brimming with soda and dump it all over him. They had mustard and ketchup fights. They lit up firecrackers on the fire escape outside, then delicately rolled them under the door, howling with glee when the explosion boomed off the walls and sent screams ripping through the audience. Whenever they spent some time watching the screen, they would cheer loudly whenever someone got beat up or shot, and make horrible screeching noises from the back of their throats during the scariest scenes. The sour old broad who served as matron would go nuts trying to grab them. She would swat and slap at them, grabbing for their ears, her eyes red, like an angry rhinoceros. But the Hawks were too slippery and too quick for her. The harder she tried to catch them, the more frantic the chase through the aisles became, until the theater itself became a wild, noisy arena.

On summer evenings, it was tougher finding things to do. Driven from the street corners, the stoops, and the parks by the older kids, they turned to torturing stray dogs and cats. Sometimes they would grab a couple of stray cats and tie them inside plastic bags. Then they would take them up on a roof, pitch them off, and listen for the thud. Peering over the edge, they would wait to see if the animal had somehow survived—listening for the sound of a squeal or a faint mew. Streak would go down and look inside the bag to see the mess that was left. Sometimes Georgie would go with him, but his stomach would turn and he would try not to look. He was always afraid that the animal would still be alive and would suddenly come shrieking out of the bag, dripping blood, and tear their throats out.

The dogs were a little tougher to push around,

because many of the strays ran in packs, living off garbage, stealing and scavenging. Even armed with sticks and bricks, the Hawks were not ready to take on a wild dog pack head on. Instead, they would try to lure a pack into chasing them. The idea was to run them right into the path of speeding traffic on some large avenue. They weren't too good at this. The dogs were too clever and a little too fast, and usually whichever frightened kid was running behind the rest and closest to the lead dog would panic and duck into an alley, followed by the entire dog pack. He would climb the first fence he could find and hang on for dear life while the dogs howled below him. The boys would have to get up on the roof of the building above and rain bricks down on the dogs until they gave up. The Hawks learned to take the dogs seriously after a while, especially after J.J. reported that he had seen the body of a junkie in an alley behind his house, with part of his face eaten away.

Georgie never brought the Hawks over to his house. He hated for people to come over. It wasn't only that his grandmother was always hovering around, muttering in Spanish, never leaving him alone. It was his mother. Her sole companion was the bottle, and, though she usually stayed conscious during the day, her strange mumblings and her way of not recognizing anyone around her made her seem crazy. Georgie always felt uncomfortable when the Hawks would trap a wino on the street and tease him and bait him, playing on his weakness. He would stand a little to the side and laugh weakly while they showed the old man a handful of change and made him beg for it. He would cringe when they finally had the old man crawling on the sidewalk, licking the pavement, and they would show him the money and then throw it into the street. They'd be laughing until the tears came, while the old guy would dash frantically into the street, searching for the coins.

What would he say if someone said to him, "Hey, man, what's with your mother?" Would he say she was sick? That she was not all there, like Blank Barnes, the mongoloid who helped out at the poolroom over on Jerome Avenue? Or that she drank too much, that she had given up on her life, that she was playing out the string with her mind swimming in alcohol. They had lived in the Bronx for a year, and Georgie wasn't sure whether she had ever been out on the Bronx streets. Most of the time, he acted as if she weren't even there. He would pass her bedroom and try not to look in. He sometimes went weeks without seeing or talking to her. As far as he was concerned, his grandmother was his only parent.

Georgie spent almost three years as a member of the Hawks. His life changed very little from year to year. During the school year, he spent as little time as he could in school, though he was careful to keep from getting into serious trouble there. During the summer, he practically lived in J.J.'s neighborhood.

But there were a few changes. Some of the Hawks moved away, and others took their place. The abandoned building they used as a clubhouse was finally torn down. But by then it didn't really matter, since they had all gotten older and were tough enough to pick a spot to hang out.

They got a little bolder, too, in the things they did. Now they raised hell on subway trains and platforms. They stole food and clothing from the little stores on Tremont Avenue whenever they could get away with it. They grabbed fruit from the outdoor stalls of the food markets, candy and gum from the dark little candy stores, polo shirts and sneakers from the bargain stores. They demanded and got small change from smaller kids who wandered into their area of Crotona Park. Through all that time, J.J. remained the kingpin, and Georgie, now thirteen, was his closest friend and his unofficial second in command.

All that changed when Georgie met the superintendent's daughter. Until then, Georgie knew very little about women. The Hawks used to imitate the older street-corner studs whenever some trim young girl would walk by; they would lick their lips and whisper and whistle and carry on. Once in a while Georgie would sneak up and peek through the stair door when his brother would take a chick up on the roof, but he couldn't see much in the dark. He just heard them whisper and giggle and moan, and generally act weird. He used to sneak a peek at his sisters whenever he could catch them naked, which wasn't often, because his grandmother was very careful about that.

One morning, Georgie went downstairs to the super's apartment to tell him one of the bathroom faucets wasn't working. His daughter answered the door. She was about a year older than Georgie, but she looked much older, and she was almost as tall as he. Her face was still young and childish, her hair was still cut in neat little rows, but her breasts and hips were already almost fully developed. He stood at the door and blinked stupidly. She asked him what he wanted. He stammered a bit and said nothing. Then she smiled at him, showing bad teeth but a nice smile, and asked him if he wanted to come in.

Slowly, over the next few weeks, she nudged Georgie toward seducing her. They worked out an elaborate scheme whereby she would let him know if her old man was home. He would knock four times on her door and then hide inside the incinerator room, leaving the door open a crack. If she knocked back or came out, he would slip inside. If she didn't, he would have to come back later. It was all he could do to keep from coming back every fifteen minutes.

He used to lie in his bed and dream up wild schemes to get her father out of the house. First he would think of breaking something or other in his own house, cause a flood in the kitchen, maybe, or break the radiator. Then the super would have to spend hours upstairs fixing it. But no, that was no good, because he would have to do it when nobody was home, and if nobody was home, then he would have to stick around while the old bastard did his repairs. Maybe he could sneak into somebody else's apartment and break something, and then sneak out? No, that was no good, because he would have to wait for someone to get home and find the mess before he could make his move. And, anyway, breaking into somebody's house was dangerous, though he was itchy enough to try it. And he would roll over on his bed, his mind reeling from his wild little schemes and his naked fantasies in a bedroom four flights down.

For months, she was all he could think of, and his life with the Hawks sputtered and finally stalled out completely. As always, J.J. would send one of his brothers over to Georgie's neighborhood to find him. Georgie was keeping his new thing a secret, though; he was afraid of what would happen if anyone found out. They might make fun of him. They might tell her father. They might try to grab her for themselves. He was angry, brooding, snappish, whenever he saw one of J.J.'s brothers. After a while, they just stopped coming around. J.J. was too proud to come by himself. For the present, Georgie just forgot about them.

So, when he wasn't downstairs in the super's bedroom, he was on his own. He would sit out on the stoop, by himself, or up on the fire escape, as he had done back in Harlem, and survey the scene. He hardly knew anyone on his own block, except for Jackie, one of his first friends from the days when he moved up to the Bronx.

Jackie was a young street hustler now, jiving and conning everyone, quick with a smile and a handslap. He would come down the street and pretend not to see Georgie until the last moment. Then he would pull sharply to a halt, step back, extend his palm, and loudly say, "What's *happening*, my man!"

"Hey, how you doin', Jackie," Georgie would reply sheepishly, gently slapping his outstretched palm.

"Where you been at, my man? I ain't seen you around but a few times, lately. Things ain't the same without Gee-boy's game."

Georgie couldn't help smiling. Jackie was always fun to be around, always exaggerating, and always ready with a fast line when his bluff was called. And Jackie was hip. He dressed cool. He could always get a bottle of wine. It was Jackie, in fact, who got Georgie his first taste of weed. They went down to the schoolyard and sat against the wire fence, taking deep puffs on a crude little joint. Georgie was thinking that he wasn't even getting off at all, when he began to feel dreamy, and the street noises and Jackie's mellow voice began to fade in and out, like a radio station that's not quite tuned in right. It was a nice feeling, like being alone in the house on a summer afternoon and hearing the sounds outside on the street for the first time. A joyful inner silence, lightly punctuated by the staccato rhythms of a crazy-quilt world.

But Jackie wasn't really what Georgie would call a friend. Georgie knew enough not to trust him. He'd sell his mother for the right price. When Georgie started buying weed from Jackie regularly, he was cheated more than once, though it took him a while to figure that out. Jackie was useful in another way, though. By watching him, Georgie began to learn how to handle himself on the street without the protection of the clique around him.

He opened his eyes for the first time to some of the street routines he had ignored before. He learned by watching, by asking a question now and then, by adding things together.

He learned about the numbers game from a conversation he overheard at the corner grocer's one afternoon. The grocer and a customer were talking about a couple of neighbors who lived around the corner—how one had been playing for twenty years and never won a dime, while the other started playing only six months before and had already hit for three winners. Georgie pieced together how it worked. A sum of money was bet on a multidigit number. The next day, or that evening, the winning number would appear in the papers. It took a while to figure out how the newspapers were involved, but finally he understood that all that mattered was that the number be different every day. He also vaguely understood that it was very difficult to win, and that the amounts paid to winners did not nearly approach what they should have been. And that somebody was making a whole lot of money, whoever it was that was collecting it.

That summer, Georgie saw a man get shot. A well-dressed man in a dark suit stepped out of his car one night and was met by another man at the entrance to a corner building. They stood and talked for a while; the conversation got louder, and they began to gesture at each other. Then there was a brilliant flash of light, and the well-dressed man fell on his knees, hung in the air briefly, and then lay down on the curb. The other man ran away. Georgie watched the whole thing from his fire escape, and it took him a while to realize what had happened. He had heard the gun go off, but the sound was muffled, so he wasn't sure what he'd heard. He sat there staring at the distant figure on the concrete, his eyes sweeping the silent street from time to time. It was late, and nobody was out. He watched for a long time, until the night sounds faded behind the noise of a distant siren. Then he climbed inside and went to sleep.

People he had never had the courage to look at before were suddenly fascinating. Junkies, for example. They always looked like they were sick or something, and Georgie could never bring himself to look at them. He didn't like to look at sick people. Now he found himself aware of every detail that made them different: the runny eyes and noses, the long-sleeved shirts that were stifling in the summer, the sleepy expressions on their faces, the monotone they used when speaking. He thought they were weird.

When he wasn't balling the super's daughter, he would go for long walks through the neighborhood by himself and check everything out. Or he would sit out on the fire escape, smoke a joint, and watch the traffic and the people go by. When the super and his daughter moved away in August, Georgie was hurt badly, even sick for a few days. But after a while he just started spending more time on his walks, or crouched down on the rough iron bars of the fire escape, watching. By the end of the summer of his thirteenth year, he was a solitary figure, maintaining little contact with anybody out on the streets. Those who knew him, and ran into him, said he had changed a lot.

It seemed natural that the newest street-gang wave would begin in the Bronx. The Bronx was the scene of the liveliest street-gang action during the late fifties, when gangs were a mandatory part of growing up. Everybody in the city knew about the Fordham Baldies: shaved monsters, crazed killers, baddest gang in the city. They liked to grab their victims and shave their heads to match their own hairless skulls, and maybe carve the initials F.B. in blood on their foreheads. Every neighborhood was thought to have a chapter of the Baldies. Rumors were always being spread that a hundred Baldies were going to crash down on this playground or that junior high and annihilate everyone.

There was more of an ethnic mix in the Bronx in the fifties, more Irish, Italian, and Polish to resent all the blacks and Puerto Ricans moving in next door. Golden Guineas, Ducky Boys, Satin Sabers—the big gangs represented every ethnic group, except that almost all had at least one black member who scared the daylights out of everyone because they knew he had to be twice as bad as everyone else to run with a white gang. The white gangs hated the black gangs, but they hated one another almost as much. Guys would sit in shop class and construct zip guns out of rusty nails and rubber bands and lead pipes, or sharpen switchblades while the teacher hid behind his newspaper.

In the parks and playgrounds, transistor radios lared out pimply little numbers with adolescent lyrics that masked the blatant sexual drive of the music —while gang members stood sinking in the soft asphalt, shimmying to the rhythm and defiantly insulting one another, one eye always nervously watching the gate in case the Baldies or some other infamous gang suddenly turned up and chased everyone home.

The kids got older, the girls got pregnant, the white families began to move away, their places taken by more blacks and Puerto Ricans. Big Daddy Dust moved in with them, and junkies nodded out on benches carved with "Donna and Desi Forever" and "Jive Bombers Are Tops." But some of the old gang members stayed on into their twenties, and on warm summer nights they would sit out on the stoop and share the old stories with the younger dudes.

The Bronx was also a natural for the new street gangs because, unlike Harlem and Bedford-Stuyvesant, there is little nighttime activity to divert everyone from just hanging out. Harlem by contrast has always been a swinging place. There are night clubs and dance halls, countless bars and after-hours spots, big movie houses, the Apollo Theater. Something is always happening in Harlem. This is true, to a lesser extent, in Bedford-Stuyvesant. But in the Bronx there are only a few fading movie houses, showing grade B movies; a few social clubs, mostly two-room store fronts with a pool table, a few booths, a bar, and a couple of flickering neon lights; a couple of local auditoriums, where a sharp young hustler could book a local group for a dance and make a few bucks:

> THE LOVE BRO GROUP PRESENTS: THE FABULOUS SENSATIONS—GUARANTEED TO SET YOUR HIPS SHAKIN', YOUR SOUL ACHIN', AND YOUR HEART BREAKIN'—TICKETS $4.00—SISTERS OVER 18 $2.00—DANCING PERMITTED—BYOB—AT THE TREMONT MANOR—FRIDAY NIGHT—YOU'LL BE FINE ON CLOUD NINE.

That's it, except for partying and hanging out. Time could be an enemy, too.

The Army was always an option. The military has traditionally serviced poor urban areas by sucking unoccupied, restless kids off the streets and into boot camp, through the draft or through recruitment policies that take advantage of kids growing up with no discernible hope of a good future. The kids grab at the slight possibility of a better life, or merely a different life, somewhere else, doing something. Thousands of street kids enlisted in some branch of the military during the Vietnam War, goaded on by promises of technical training and a highly paid military career, or a marketable skill that would later pay well in civilian life. Later, they would find themselves shipped out as scarecrows for the Viet Cong. Hundreds more would go through basic training, come home on leave, and disappear, AWOL, into the concrete when their orders for Vietnam arrived. That meant that getting a job was doubly hard, since draft status was an important factor then.

The Vietnam War also managed to make heroin cheap and available for those who had never dreamed of trying it back on Eastchester Avenue. Those who didn't die, suffer crippling wounds, or return addicted, or psychological wrecks, returned to the street two or three years older and just as unemployable. Returning veterans, possessing deadly new skills, still experiencing the bitter taste of the war, and realizing that nobody back home gave a damn about them, formed the nucleus for the new gang wave.

The romantic militancy of the Young Lords and Black Panthers played a part in gang formation, too. Panthers and Lords came on as people who were proud not only of the color of their skin and their cultural heritage, but also of themselves as individuals. Dressed all in black, bullets wound about their bodies, automatic rifles resting casually in their hands, they talked with melodious toughness, not merely defiant but openly hostile. They made the other side cringe and back down and give in. They told others what to do, and those others—doctors, lawyers, politicians, even cops—listened; they were afraid to do anything else. It was a revelation on the street.

Many kids who are in street gangs today have cousins or older brothers or uncles who were in the Panthers or the Lords during 1969–1970. Other new gangs were forming in the South Bronx during that time. Many of the leaders of these new gangs were former Panthers or Lords themselves. They left for various reasons: because the discipline was too tough or the rhetoric too confusing, or because real revolution was a bit more than they had bargained for. A five-to-one stomping makes sense on the street; a gun battle with the police where getting killed was the most likely outcome made no sense at all.

The fusion of all these elements came late in 1969. All the Vietnam vets and AWOL Army dropouts were hanging out. The regular crop of school dropouts were hanging out. The militant dropouts were hanging out. All had ingested at least a mild dose of militant pride, the solidarity of blackness, the machismo of Latinos. Now it was "Hey, brother," not "Hey, man." And maybe somebody said, Let's get our own thing together here, get uniforms and, shit, live like brothers and such, clean the neighborhood out, get the junkies and pushers out, chase the honkie thieves away.

Guns were available all over, everything from .22's and .38's to M–16's. Someone would take a trip upstate, or down south to North Carolina or Kentucky or Tennessee, and come back with a bagful of handguns. Many vets had come back with weapons as souvenirs of their service time. By late 1969, tough and gaudy street cliques were sprouting up all over the southern and eastern portions of the Bronx, in an area stretching north and east from 138th Street up Southern Boulevard to Hoe Avenue, and into the Hunts Point section.

Leaders of these gangs were older than gang leaders today. Most of them were in their late teens or early twenties; many of them had already served time in prison. Some of the big names were Spanish Tony of the Bachelors, Black Tony of the Savage Skulls, Power and Butter of the Majestic Warlocks, Black Benjie of the Savage Nomads, and Robert Williams of the Peacemakers. Like their predecessors in the Fordham Baldies or the Golden Guineas, they were as razor-blade tough as the street rumors claimed they were. They had seen shootings and stabbings long before they ever put on their colors. The members of their gangs were also usually older, sometimes actually friends made in prison or in the Army.

At first the gangs directed their attention to drug traffic, waging a private war on pushers big and small, enacting and sometimes enforcing, with a vengeance, strict hard-drug taboos on their memberships. Their method of operation was simple. Junkies were accosted in hallways and alleyways. They were beaten severely and then warned to pass the word: junkies and pushers, move out. This accomplished little. Then a few junkies would be tossed off rooftops or down elevator shafts, or shot in the face, or stabbed in the groin. By early 1970, the gangs had partially succeeded in pushing drug traffic west across Third Avenue.

This kind of vigilantism did not go unnoticed, even if the victims were junkies. By 1970, the police department was taking more than a casual glance at the street gangs. By then, many of the gangs had moved from anti-drug militancy into the vacuum of power that the pushers had left behind. But the territorial lines of control were never formally drawn. At least a half dozen cliques were hanging around on the corners near Bruckner Boulevard and Hoe Avenue, each one with a notion of controlling the area. Any incident—an insult to somebody's girl, a harmless but insulting piece of graffiti, the wearing of gang colors on the wrong block—could provoke a shooting, and some sixteen-year-old would be found with half his head blown away.

•

Snoopy was once a gang leader. He was once a soldier, too. He learned how to use a gun in the Marines, and then he used it some more when he got back to the Bronx. It was probably the thing he knew how to do best in the world.

When Snoopy was growing up, the other kids called him "faggot" and "maricón" and beat him up when they weren't making a fool of him. Every day on the way home from school, something would happen to Snoopy. They would steal his shoes. Or they would throw his books down the sewer. Or they would bury him in the back of the bus, where no one could hear his screams above the noise, and just beat on him until they all got off the bus. Then he would have to get out and ride another bus back to his stop.

When Snoopy was seventeen, he decided to join the Marines. He needed to learn how to take care of himself. He had had enough of being dumped on and humiliated. He worked hard in boot camp. His body toughened up. He learned how to use a variety of different weapons, from handguns and knives to hand grenades and automatic rifles.

The others respected him. He was as tough as anyone in camp. He didn't make friends easily, though. He didn't like to talk to other people. They made him angry. They were always trying to be funny at his expense. The others kept away from him, and he liked it that way. Let them think he was crazy.

Snoopy went to Vietnam. He was anxious to get there. It was a chance to make up for all those years, a chance to prove he was as much of a man as the next guy. He volunteered for all the dangerous patrols. He wanted a chance at shooting some people.

In Vietnam, Snoopy shot a lot of people. He thought he was doing great. But the Army didn't think so. He wasn't too good at following orders. And they also seemed to think that there were times that he shot people when he really didn't have to. Bullshit, Snoopy thought. If they didn't want him to kill people, why'd they bring him over here and give him a gun?

The Army sent him home. They weren't particularly angry at him. They just didn't want him using an M–16 any more. He got an honorable discharge, with a notation that he had been released early for psychological reasons. All it meant was that Snoopy would have a hard time getting a job if his prospective employer happened to look at his military record.

Unless he wanted a job killing people. Which was all he had learned to do in the Army.

When Snoopy came back to the Bronx, there were all these guys on the street, wearing these weird jackets with designs on the back. The jackets looked like . . . like uniforms, only they were cool. He liked the way these studs kind of pushed everybody around on the street. People respected them because they had to respect them. It wasn't that different from Vietnam.

Snoopy joined the Black Spades. They were one of the biggest gangs around. A lot of the guys in the Spades had been in prison or had fought in Vietnam. But none of them had killed as many men as Snoopy had.

Snoopy rose fast in the Spades. He earned a reputation as a kamikaze-type dude, the one crazy guy that other gangs learn to watch out for. The Spades made him their War Lord. He was the guy who did the negotiating with the other gangs. He was also the guy who made sure there were enough guns to go around. The Spades used him mostly as a hit man.

With Snoopy as War Lord, the Spades started knocking over other South Bronx gangs like so many young trees in a hurricane. Snoopy had a favorite way of intimidating another gang. He would arrange for a peace meeting. Two members of the Spades and two members of the other gang would attend with Snoopy choosing the spot where they would meet. While the meeting was in progress, Snoopy would slip in unnoticed and sneak up behind the two rival gang members. Then he would place the barrel of a sawed-off shotgun to their heads. Then they would all sign a peace treaty. They must have believed he would pull the trigger.

Once, another gang decided to call his bluff. They had two cars outside, full of gang members armed and waiting. When Snoopy walked outside, they opened fire. He dived behind a parked car and returned the fire with his shotgun. He reloaded and waited. Then he dashed out into the street, rolled over a couple of times, and fired both barrels point blank through one of the car windows. The other car drove away. Wham. Blam. Just like boot camp.

Snoopy was busted for attempted murder four times in six months. That didn't account for all the times he wasn't caught, or the dudes he claimed he shot who didn't recover. The third time he was up on an attempted murder rap, the judge and the probation officer suggested psychiatric help. They thought he was crazy. So crazy that they didn't even want to put him on probation. They figured that if he had to report to a psychiatrist and a probation officer at the same time, and he felt any kind of conflict about them at any time, he might try to kill one or both of them. They released him in the custody of his lawyer, who worked for a local drug rehabilitation program.

It took ten days for the right psychiatrist to be found. The court called the lawyer and asked him to bring his client back. But they were too late. Snoopy was in jail again, on another attempted murder rap.

This time, they put him in prison, where he wouldn't get to shoot at anybody again—for almost two years.

V

After the pushers ran west, the gangs turned on any available target. Landlords and storekeepers were shaken down, neighborhood residents got tapped for periodic contributions to the gang's treasury, youths who were not gang members were subjected to endless, demeaning street confrontations, where the slightest resistance could result in a beating or a stabbing that could mean a week in the hospital.

Gangs at this time had a membership that was generally older, wilder and more independent than the later gangs. Members did not for the most part live at home anymore. Some were fresh out of juvenile prisons and found that the gang was a perfect outlaw family to join. Others were returnees from Vietnam. A few months of job seeking or toying with the notion of returning to school was sufficiently frustrating to make them fall back on hanging out. Still others were junkies who had dried the dust out of their blood. Many early gangs strictly enforced anti-drug taboos, and members who had joined while still carrying a habit cut it loose cold with a gang brother sitting shotgun during the whole horrible trip.

The word spread like a shot of Puerto Rican rum in the blood. All over the Bronx, people were talking about the crazy dudes in the South Bronx. They would show up at parties in groups of two or three, with those bad, bad jackets and a studied way of walking and talking that informed all but the highest and dumbest not to mess with them. The Bronx was the kind of place where, in every neighborhood, somebody had a cousin or a half brother or a nephew living in another neighborhood. So every neighborhood clique had a tieline to this new gang thing that was happening in the South Bronx.

Gang fever spread like a tenement fire. New gangs were formed from every group of more than a half dozen kids who lived on the same block. Some invented their own names. Some took on the names of parent gangs (central divisions, they were called) in the South Bronx. The larger gangs divided up into age groups. Pre-teeners formed junior divisions. When they got older, and after undergoing a brutal initiation or carrying out a dangerous assignment designated by the the senior gang president, they graduated into membership in the regular gang. Gang presidents often used younger members to do the shooting when someone was to be killed. That way, if the police arrested several gang members for the murder, the kid would confess and get off with a sentence to a juvenile home.

There was, too, a place for former gang members in their twenties or early thirties. Power and Butter, once legendary presidents of the Majestic Warlocks, became, in their early twenties, members of a group called the Old Timers, which served as a kind of council of elders to the Warlocks.

Women's auxiliary units were formed, with names like the Satin Ladies and the Ghetto Sisters. Their functions varied according to gang structure. In black gangs, the women were often every bit as tough and played as much of a policy-making role as did the men. In Puerto Rican gangs, the women performed mostly menial tasks and sometimes were treated as collective sexual property by gang members. Some gang presidents like Black Benjie would make a fetish of keeping a stable of "wives." Before he was shot and killed in a gang fight, he had boasted that he was going to form a gang tribe and raise dozens of his own children within the gang structure.

The big South Bronx central division gangs were a thing apart from the smaller neighborhood cliques that began sporting colors throughout the Bronx. The South Bronx was for more than a year in a state of perpetual siege. Gang alliances and animosities changed so often that members had trouble keeping track and would often fight with anyone who wore colors different from their own. The mass confrontation between the total memberships of two gangs and their allies, armed with chains, sticks, pipes, brass knuckles, even rocks, in a playground or on an open field or empty lot—the rumble that was the classic form of gang war in the late fifties—was abandoned.

In its place were ambushes, gangland style execu-
tions, firebombings and kidnappings. Protection
money from local store owners was not demanded
merely through intimidation; store owners were
robbed repeatedly, their windows smashed night
after night, their stores firebombed, their cars stolen
and destroyed. When full-scale territorial war was
declared, no one was safe. Kids bicycling home from
school would be stopped in broad daylight and questioned about which gang they favored. Any answer
was likely to result in the victim's being shot or
stabbed. A wino who once smashed in the window of
a Savage Nomad storefront headquarters was shot
five times and, with two cinderblocks tied to his
shoulders, thrown off a rooftop. The South Bronx
gangs resembled gangs of the twenties and thirties
more than they did the comparatively tame gangs of
the fifties.

Newer gangs springing up in other sections of
the Bronx were not nearly so violent. They tended to
be more sedentary, more concerned with protecting
their own turf from marauding gangs than with controlling wide areas. The smaller gangs controlled territories of three to four blocks; by contrast, some of
the South Bronx gangs sought domination over three
to four square miles of turf. Members of the newer
gangs were younger and talked a lot tougher than
their experience could back up. Fights between the
smaller gangs rarely involved weapons, at least at
first. The sight of a gun or the sound of a shot would
send everyone scurrying home.

But raw competition was what it was about—

fighting and winning and being the best at something. By age sixteen, a gang member would have been through his first war. He would have seen a friend stagger down the street in crazy circles, holding his stomach to keep his guts from falling out where a knife had gone in. He might have suffered a broken hand or a busted nose, been slashed across the face or razor-cut on his chest. He might have smashed somebody's skull with a rock again and again, until the rock was damp with blood and the head seemed oddly shapeless.

Big Walter of the Bachelors did five years for armed robbery and was involved in most of the big wars between the Secret and Imperial Bachelors and the other South Bronx street gangs. He says that no matter how mad he got, how crazy afterward, he remembered the ones he cut, or shot, or even just stomped. He would feel good when it was over, he says, if he came out okay and was not hurt too badly; but he would remember the fight later, and that's when he would get scared. Because he knew it could have been him.

VI

Georgie started snorting dope about midway through his fourteenth year. It scared him, doing that; it moved his head around a whole lot more than the weed he'd been smoking. It was a big year for wine, cheap wine. A couple of dozen brands of what tasted like fermented cherry Coke sold in large volume everywhere—Thunderbird, Ripple, Bali Hai. So Georgie tipped the bottle for a whole summer, feeling pretty nice, checking out the ladies, singing in a hoarse croak at the top of his lungs in time with the tinny transistors blaring from open windows, or feeling hot asphalt through the rubber soles of his sneakers as he rocked back and forth on his heels, playing infield in a stickball game. It was a fine summer—he ran sweating in the sun and the hot breezes all day and partied every night. He knew everyone. He ran through half a dozen chicks that summer, after a year of suffering through long stretches of fear and embarrassment in the face of the tough, haughty young chicks at the junior high.

And he had lots of friends, guys he played ball with all day—stickball, football, basketball, handball. Friends from school, from the neighborhood, from the old Hawks. He and J.J. were tight again. They went everywhere together, movies, pizza, ball games, Rye Beach. He forgot the cold winter months spent indoors, talking to no one, watching serials on TV day after day, or walking the streets outside, wandering nowhere. He forgot the dreary days at school, sitting in the cramped wooden desks, staring out the window or carving doodles in the wood. He forgot how he had had almost no friends that first year. The summer had changed all that.

Now with the first cool changes of September, the hot summer streets began to empty out, and Georgie felt a choking dread building inside him. He couldn't stand the thought of going through another winter like the last one. When the school year began, Georgie couldn't drag himself out of bed and off to school. His grandmother would shake him and shout at him and mutter at him. Once his sister had poured a glass of cold water on him. He tore out of bed and grabbed her in a rage. His grandmother had come charging in with a bottle in her hand, shrieking incoherently, ready to brain him.

His grandmother gave up after a few weeks. Georgie would lie in bed, eyes open, listening to the sounds of the morning as they drifted through his half dreams: truck rattles and auto coughs, voices chatting, arguing, coming from every direction in every pitch. Doorbells, now close, now far away, doors creaking, then slamming shut. The TV set, a reassuring blur of noise until the commercials came on. Then every word was suddenly annoyingly crisp. And the radio playing the sentimental Spanish songs his grandmother listened to in the morning.

He would lie there, gradually waking up, hoping each day to sleep the sunlight away. And always failing, until, around noon, he would drag himself out of bed and make himself a cup of coffee. He would sit staring at the dark black liquid and draw slowly and absently on cigarette after cigarette, never saying a word, as his grandmother flitted in and out. Early in the afternoon, his grandmother would say, "I'm going out now; you want anything?" and he would say "No," his voice creaky and flat. More than a month passed, and, except for a few trips to the store for cigarettes and food, he never left the house.

On one trip to the store, he ran into a chick he had played around with during the summer. He asked her about some of the people they had both known during the summer, when they all hung out at the high school yard some ten blocks away from Georgie's house. She told him that most of them were going to school over on the other side of Crotona Park, that they all hung out over that way. He slapped her on the bottom and continued on his way. He thought nothing of it.

On a weekday morning a week later, Georgie got out of bed and dressed quickly. His grandmother was stunned at first, then she asked where he was going, and he said, "Out." He didn't know where he was going. But when he got outside, he paused to suck in the cold morning air and think about what to do. He no longer felt the same gnawing emptiness. He felt better now; after a few minutes of savoring his mood, he headed for the bus stop. He was going to head across the park and find out what was happening on the other side.

•

Georgie didn't know why he got hooked on dope. He did some serious snorting when he began to hang with the Crotona Park kids. A lot of them started with skag early on. A lot of them later got strung out for good. There was no one to blame, really, no pusher dude with a slimy grin saying, "Here, kid, try some of this." No bunch of guys standing around saying, "Hey, look at the jive faggot, he's scared to try this shit, probably afraid his cock will fall off." The stuff was around, guys were doing it, and so he tried it, thinking, no harm, man, everybody does it, and they feel good. Some guys would tell him it was great for screwing. Just grab a fox and some dust and go up somewhere private; you could screw your brains out on the stuff and never get tired. But kids say that about a lot of things.

Hanging out in the park were some older studs, fifteen and sixteen years old, who talked about getting high all the time, about putting on a nice head every morning, about how you could get so you could goof on the whole world. You could laugh at everything, see the straights for the cruel joke the world was playing on them. So, one afternoon, sitting in somebody's parked car, listening to a couple of older guys talking, he took the little spoon from one of them and sucked a couple of crystals up into his nostril, in a hurry, because he was afraid of waiting too long and looking like a fool. He was already nice and tight, wined up good, and he just blasted right out, nodded out for fifteen minutes or so, the others not even noticing, until someone said, "Hey, look, man, Georgie just tipped," and everyone laughed at the green kid in the back seat asleep with his mouth wide open and his nostrils moving in and out with every breath.

It was no big deal after all. Even after he came to, he didn't think it was such a big deal. But he felt older, more experienced. He was pleased with the casual way he had been offered a snort, and his blasé manner of accepting it. It was weeks before he even tried the stuff again. He was still young; he had no steady connection; he had little money; he was for the most part content to grab a little weed and get high once in a while, buy the cheap wine and pass it around in a circle while everybody told stories of past summers. Sometimes they would sit on the cracked benches in the park and goof on all the people passing through; nervous, most of them, skulking by those kids, staring straight ahead, a lot of them with hands in their pockets, grasping wallets tightly, or clutching handbags under their armpits like footballs.

"Hey, Georgie, ain't that your mother, man? What do you mean, no, man; I ought to know. I was

out with her last night. Hey, lady, ain't you this turkey's mother? C'mon, lady, answer when I'm talking to you."

For all his new friends, Georgie was still uncomfortable and nervous. It was a big burden, now that he wasn't going to school anymore, to think of something to do every day. On top of that, his grandmother was hip to what was going on. She wasn't dropping a penny of the hard-earned welfare money she had fought for years to keep on this lazy devil who was too young to work but so smart he didn't have to go to school. And, big as he was at fourteen, it wasn't easy to sneak onto the subway or hitch bus rides anymore. Many days, when the weather wasn't bad, Georgie just walked the two miles or so to the other side of the park. When the weather was bad, he would stay in and watch the soaps with his grandmother. It was better than just lying up in the bed; but after a while, he began to get itchy for a change.

In the spring, one of the guys over in the park asked Georgie if he would like to make some money helping to move some furniture the next day. He shrugged his shoulders and said why not. He was, in fact, overjoyed. This was his first job. He finally would get some cash to roll around in his pocket. Georgie, the kid, and the kid's brother worked in a beat-up old fourteen-foot Chevy truck, a blue crate precariously balanced on the back of a grizzled cab. They moved Puerto Rican families from one tenement to another, from Morrisania to University Heights, from Parkchester to Hunts Point, charging them a hundred dollars for a full day's work. Out of this, Georgie got fifteen. He worked on the average about four days a week, although there were weeks when they didn't need him at all. Once he worked a six-day week. When he came home that Saturday night, he kept pulling all the bills out to look at and count over and over again.

The money made a big difference in Georgie's life. His first impulse was to start spending money on clothes, on a portable radio, on a stereo, on records. He dreamed of saving up hundreds, maybe even thousands of dollars, owning a fast car in a few years, a rich man while his friends were still playing boys' games in the playground. The first thing he did was to start giving his grandmother some of that money every week. She cried the first time he did that. His brothers had never contributed a dime to the house. Both of them had moved out and left the family on its own. If Georgie was giving her money, he must be stealing it. She pleaded with him to tell her the truth and to stop stealing. It took Georgie a whole night of yelling, then cajoling, then speaking in a soft whisper when she stopped weeping, to convince her that he was really working, that the money was really his. She cried even more when she finally believed him. He went to bed that night feeling like a man.

The rest of the money just burned right through his pockets. He had some good times. He saw just about every movie in the Bronx. The wine and beer was on him almost all the time. He bought himself a black velvet cap and a mahogany cane, which he sported whenever he went out on weekends. Every Friday night, he would hunt down a connection and buy a dime bag from him. Then he would grab the bus and head across the park for the party of the week.

By the summer he was snorting heroin about once a week. He still wasn't giving it much thought. He wasn't buying much himself, though he often offered to pay for his share. He began to look forward to that first rush, the easy wave of sleepy numbness that washed over him, soothing the week's aches and pains, slowing the brain down, mellowing everything. Sometime—he didn't remember when—he decided to buy a large amount on his own, as another way of proving what a generous and heavy brother he really was. He bought several nickel bags and took them with him to the parties. He then started buying in larger quantities. He wanted more for himself, so he could get off on his own once in a while. He started bringing it with him wherever he went. Sometimes, when he was working, he would disappear while they were eating lunch and do a quick snort. It made him feel calm and cool and on top of everything. It got so he was spending more and more money on skag. When this bothered him, he stopped buying for everyone and kept it all to himself. He even considered not giving his grandmother any money, but he figured that would be too much of a hassle.

There came a time, during the summer, when he just couldn't get off by snorting anymore. He knew guys who skinpopped, he knew some who shot up, but he had always been afraid of the needle and the habit. But, hell, he didn't feel addicted now. And what was the use of buying the stuff if he didn't get high off it? He got his first needle from a little man who lived on his corner and worked as an orderly in a nursing home. Ten minutes later, he climbed up the stairs to the roof of his building and went behind the door, next to the elevator shaft. The needle was full of the liquid he had prepared on the stove downstairs, while his grandmother was out shopping. The only sounds he could hear as he rolled up his sleeve were the creaky elevator machinery churning and straining and his own heart beating and throbbing. They both seemed to stop when he poked the needle home.

About a month later the old blue truck finally gave out, and Georgie was out of a job.

There are all different kinds of junkies. All sizes, shapes, classes. There are junkies who got hooked on morphine in a Veterans Hospital during World War II and have been on heroin ever since. There are Chinese junkies who have been doing opium since their teenage days in the old country, and are so straight they'll look down on anyone who collects unemployment benefits. There are junkies back from Vietnam who got hooked when they smoked what they thought was powdered Vietnamese marijuana, and didn't discover the truth until they went on rest and rehabilitation leave and started going through withdrawal. There are junkies with M.D. licenses who, thanks to their special privilege, can lead normal, productive professional lives and can nod out three times a day besides. There are junkies who think it's the heroin they're on, but find out through some quirk that it's really the needle; they just have to shoot something. There are others who are addicted to depressants; they may get off junk and go on barbiturates or even black-market methadone, or they may rehabilitate completely and become a more socially acceptable alcoholic. There are junkies, former soldiers, who could get a day's supply of ninety-four-percent pure heroin in Saigon for a few dollars, without the Army's finding out about it or detecting any difference in their performance. Some won their medals, then came back and tried to get the stuff on the street, only to find that they couldn't even get off on the dope being sold back home. They were forced into a situation where they had to have a fabulous income to maintain the habit they had acquired so cheaply in the service. One veteran, now in a Bronx drug clinic, was a trained Special Forces soldier in Vietnam for more than two years. He was a highly skilled, jungle-hardened killer with a closet heroin habit. When he came back, he found that there was no way to keep up without channeling his skills into professional crime. He became a top-flight cat burglar. With a pair of Converse sneakers and supple leather gloves, he could climb to the roof of a building by simply grasping the spaces between the bricks on either side of the narrow space that separates many New York apartment buildings. He claimed to have committed more than 250 burglaries during a nine-month binge, before getting caught and being remanded to the drug rehabilitation center. He was always heavily armed, and he thinks that if someone had ever interrupted him in mid-mission, he would have killed him. He proved so intelligent and highly motivated that, within a year, he had climbed through the ranks of the drug program to leadership position as a resident counselor on a paid salary.

A sizable number of street pushers are addicts themselves; pushing is a great problem solver in a lot of ways. First, the money factor; the mark-up on the wholesale dope that he buys makes more than the difference for the dope he uses himself. His connection is usually more reliable; he is, after all, part of the corporation and not just another crummy customer. His big disadvantage is that his clientele is likely to be limited to his contacts in the neighborhood. He is going to try to turn everybody from six to ninety on to dope. He and others like him constitute by far the largest number of police arrests for pushing. He is guilty of a multitude of sins, from cutting his product with poisonous substances to mercilessly hounding some poor bastard who has just dried out on Rikers Island into getting high again. He entertains grandiose notions of making the big sale someday, of graduating someday to the executive superfly level, surrounded by skag and coke and all manner of exotic drugs, women, jewelry, cars, anything the papers or movies were currently glamorizing.

There used to be a junkie in the northeast section of the Bronx, just south of Coop City, who was a well-liked, harmless sort, a butt for neighborhood jokes, the kind who could always hustle up a few bucks because everyone felt sorry for him—the suicidal type, who might jump off a roof one night if he couldn't get up the nerve or strength to knock off an empty apartment and raise enough bread for a day's worth of white bags. One winter night a few years ago, he copped some money from his mother and went downtown to 149th Street to hit his cousin for some heroin he had just received. He made his transaction, and grabbed the train for the ride back home. But he was anxious, almost horny, for this dope, because the Far East stuff is five, six, ten times stronger than the stuff on the streets here. He couldn't wait for a comfortable bathroom at home. He couldn't wait for a warm stairwell at the top of an apartment building. He couldn't even wait to get out of the subway station. When he got to his stop, he walked quickly into the dingy bathroom, put a dime into a stall, clicked the door shut, took out the loaded needle he had already prepared and shot in the happy juice. He knew enough to get the hell out, though, so he packed up his things and started to leave. He had hardly taken a couple of steps before the first rush hit him like an electric tidal wave and bounced his mind off the brownish yellow tiles behind him. His body began to wave back and forth, as if he were some skinny young tree helpless in the face of a strong gust of wind. He staggered to a corner of the room, and there, behind a couple of large orange steel cans, like a puppet with its strings cut, he collapsed at the knees and, with a steel pipe as his pillow, fell into a long, languishing nod.

Nothing unusual about that, as junkie stories go, except that his pillow was actually a steampipe. He had hidden himself well enough to escape being seen by the one or two night-shift workers who might have wandered in during the night, so that he slept his nod away into the morning. He slowly began to wake up in the middle of a strange nightmare. He was burning, and the smell of his own flesh was in his nose, but it had melted, and he was turning into liquid, and becoming cemented into the thing that was burning him. He awoke to a giant stab of pain and smoke, tiny wafts of it drifting before his eyes. Twice he tried to scream but could only croak. Then he gathered his strength and screamed louder. One of the men in the token booth rushed in and found him. The right side of his face was a mass of raw, steaming flesh. "Fucking crazy junkies," the man said, and left to call an ambulance.

The kid lived, his face a constant reminder to anyone who could stand to look at him of just how low a human being could get by shooting dope. And there were others, such as the pathetic women wearing halter tops and ridiculously short skirts, trying vacantly to attract a trick. Even the most desperate of men couldn't look at the pockmarked legs and puffed cheeks and hands without some feeling of revulsion. But there are streets, neighborhoods where there are so many human wrecks, ravaged by dope, that it begins to matter less and less. The more you see, the more unreal it all becomes, like staring at a red brick tenement wall for hours on end and trying to think of it as home.

For a kid growing up on the street, the social pressure becomes unbearable enough to make some form of escape necessary. The pressure is not to succeed along some established career route but rather to claim your own humanity and worth in a world that measures worth and humanity by standards you can't begin to approach. How can you think of becoming a lawyer when you've never really learned to read? How can you plan for tomorrow if you can't control today?

So you try to make it in the world in which you find yourself. You try to crack the social hierarchies, bowing to the arbitrary and rigid nature of each segment religiously lest you be ruthlessly excluded and sometimes even hounded out of the neighborhood as a "lame." The strongest learn to feed off the weakest, drawing power and status from their domination. The girls are as ruthless as the boys, possibly more so, since they can exert power cross-sexually in more instances than males can. There are similar hierarchical systems in every adolescent group, but the physical degradation and mental hostility encountered by a ghetto reject, who has already been rejected by most of society, is by far the most devastating.

And when the days hanging out on the street corner begin to get longer and more empty; when the wine and the partying and the constant banter of insults isn't fun anymore, or hurts too much; when the pressure to get a job or just to get out of the house seems to increase by the day; and when the frustrations which hold you away from control of your own life begin to tell you that perhaps you are worth somewhat less than others in the world, that your humanity is less precious, then, suddenly, being a junkie isn't so bad after all. The sharp, cold needle with the warm, oozy gift of dreams inside that gives you the power to forget makes things all right again. The gnawing feeling that has swelled within you like a great shadow touching every aspect of your life, every private corner of your soul, the feeling that you have failed as a human being, is eased. You're a junkie now, and whatever you do, no matter how low you sink, it's no longer your fault. In a strange, terrifying way, you have given away your life to save your humanity.

The trap is sprung, the search is ended. No more nervous pacing on the streets or anxious waiting on the corners, wondering what to do next—searching, hoping for something different, something new, something with a future. Big Daddy Dust takes over; you on the street corner now, brother, best be looking to cop some bread, you got no time to run your rap down to every neat little trick coming down the street; you got a car, you sell that turkey 'cause you gonna need the dough.

The first sensation is one of revelation. The answer is here, by God, you've never felt so goddamn good; floating, above the drivel—free at last. The first crash to consciousness is not rough; you come out in dreamy stages, and the memory of the experience stays with you, leaving behind a taste of a very private place of total calm, of deep, soft, untroubled and uninterrupted sleep. Then there is that very prideful sense of strength. You're not hooked on this shit, you can take it or leave it, maybe do a snort every once in a while at a party, or in the schoolyard, just to recapture that good feeling, but there is no compulsion coursing through your veins. You're a mean stud, not like the trash down the street. They look like zombies, man, eyes running, the whites streaked with red, nose swollen at the nostrils, scabbed over, dirty most of the time. You see them, but all the same, you want to do it again; which is cool because, after all, it has no hold on you, you can take it or leave it; you just like the way it feels. You start to cop a bag and snort some crystals once a week; in the stairwell, near the door to the roof, where no one can see you and no one will pass you, and you just drift right out that door and into the cold sky above, only it's warm up there, and there is nothing below or above. Which is nice. But the high is never quite the same as that first time, that first sweet feeling of discovery. And soon it becomes boring, another disappointment, another broken promise.

It becomes very important to recapture the first time, to reach the right jolt, the one that set you totally free. Now it's once a day you've got to do those crystals, and if no one is around, you do it by yourself, in your room when no one is home, or in the toilet stall at school, sitting on the cold seat, pants down, like you're really using the john. You learn to splash a little cold tap water on your nose when you come out, so that no one will notice your swollen and distended nostrils. You get nervous when you can't cop, restless, agitated, irritated, upset sometimes. Goddamn, if they'd only stop selling such lousy stuff, if you could only cop some really dynamite stuff, and a lot of it, stuff that could really get you off, why, then, you wouldn't do it so damn much. Nagging at you from the back of your mind is the gnawing fear that it is happening to you, that you're hooked. But you fight that fear with a mental strength juiced up by desperation. You cannot admit that it might be true, because then you would have to stop, have to get help, and you don't want to stop, not now, and you don't dare think of why not.

Finally, you're shooting the stuff three times a week, but just don't get off, it's just another high. You start thinking needle, seeing it in the mind's eye, choking on it, gagging on it, pushing it away. But it stays there, bright and slim and streamlined and full of promise, full and ripe, bursting and bulging with happy sauce. You turn over on your bed and try to bury your brain in your pillow to shut out the light and turn off the movie.

But in the morning, whenever that is, the needle is still there, bright as day now, and innocent, the sharp point a little smaller now, the bulb end fatter; there is some dynamite boiled down and packed inside that glass. Stay behind that, brother, and you won't be riding on no damn cloud; you'll rocket right the fuck out of here, out into black, black space, a goddamn outlaw spaceman.

But still, in the back of your mind is the fear that burns pale but strong: what if you rocket right out and never come back? No blood, only a limp, lifeless bag of limbs, mouth open in flaccid stupidity, the empty tube still cradled in your fingers, loosely. OD, OD, OD, everybody talks about it. "Where's Freddy been, man? I ain't seen him around." "Oh man, didn't you hear, Freddy's been here and gone, baby;

cat found him cold as the night over in the schoolyard by the fence. He OD'd, man."

But the decision is not yours to make anymore.

*A story. A boy visits his older brother in the
hospital. The brother is an addict, he has overdosed,
he has barely missed the ultimate nod. The boy has
been told that his brother was on a long journey, that
he was hurt and almost didn't come back, but that
he will be all right, now.*

"Where did you go?" the boy asks.

"Uh . . . far, far away," his brother answers.

"Who did you see?"

"Well . . . I saw God."

"What did He say?"

"He said . . . 'later.'"

Of those close to Georgie, it was J.J. who first noticed
that he was getting strung out on dope. J.J. and Georgie were inseparable during the summer, but when
the school term started, they didn't see much of each
other. Georgie had stopped going to school al-
together. J.J. was angling for a basketball scholarship
to a school out west, and he did most of his hanging
out around the high school.

When Georgie stopped coming around, J.J.
wasn't surprised. He figured they were each into different things now. After a month or more, though, he
started wondering why Georgie wasn't coming
around at all, not even just to see what was happening. Could be a woman, he thought, thinking back to
the old days, but Georgie was sixteen, not thirteen,
and a woman wouldn't do this to him anymore. J.J.
was busy, though, with practice and such, so he
didn't give much thought to it.

He was playing in a half-court game over at Crotona Park one day. His squad went down, 10–8, and with a twenty-minute wait for another shot at the court, he figured it was time to make it home. On his way back, he saw Georgie sitting alone on a bench.

"Hey man, where you been hiding? How you doin'?" he said in surprise.

Georgie looked up at him sleepily. He didn't seem to recognize who it was. Then he blinked and smiled slightly.

"Hey, J.J., what's happenin'?"

"Where you been keeping yourself, man?"

"Oh, you know, around, man."

There was an awkward silence. Georgie closed his eyes and squirmed a bit. J.J. was irritated and decided not to say anything else. The silence grew and hung more awkwardly.

"I'll catch you later, man," J.J. said slowly. He started to walk away, carefully at first, and then faster as he got angrier. Fuck that jive turkey, he thought to himself.

A few days later, J.J. saw Georgie hanging out with another guy he knew from the neighborhood. J.J. knew for a fact that the dude was a pusher. And then it slowly dawned on him. The red, swollen eyes, almost weepy, watery. His dull conversation and slow recognition. Shit, he thought, Georgie is a god-damn dope fiend.

He almost decided to do something about it. Georgie had drifted in and out of his life, but he was probably still his closest and oldest friend. He brooded about it for days, even during practice, catching a heavy lecture on paying attention from his coach and almost being suspended from the team. It was then that he decided just to forget about it. Colleges don't give basketball scholarships to niggers who hang out with junkies, he reasoned. Maybe Georgie was just snorting. Anyway, it was Georgie's problem.

Georgie was shooting up pretty regularly by then, about once a day. He had stayed away from it for a few weeks, especially when he lost his job. But he panicked when he thought about not being able to buy dope at all, so much so that he lost his nerve and copped a bag and shot up immediately, behind a tree in the park. After that, he started making the rounds of all the people he knew in the park, begging money and a little white dust, trying to get together odd bags of skag wherever he could expect a welcome.

Those welcomes got fewer and fewer as he made the rounds more frequently. They were all borderline junkies anyway, hanging on by a thread of their own fear, and they knew the signs of someone whose thread had snapped. His pleading got more and more desperate. He asked for more and more money each time he came around, and he was never uptight about the money he owed from the last time. When reminded, he would smile vacantly and say, "Yeah, right man, I know, but you know I'm good for it, soon as I can get a gig together." And petulant: "You don't have to hassle me, man, you dig. If you ain't got the bread, just lighten up."

His friends started to avoid him when they could, and ignore him when they couldn't avoid him. He would walk up to a bunch of guys standing at a water fountain. He would greet them loudly, and they would glance at him stonefaced and go on with what they were saying. Every time he would interrupt someone to say something, he would be greeted with the same icy glances. Finally someone would say, "Later," and they would all drift away, leaving him standing there alone.

He was in a horrible bind. He needed money to keep doing his dope. He was convinced that if he could only be certain he could cop each day, he could hold his habit down to a needle a day. To get the bread, though, he needed a job. He had nothing to get a job with but a ninth-grade education. He thought of going the program route and getting a job through one of the dozens of government agencies that offered jobs to street dropouts. But he was afraid they might find out about his habit, especially when he was so strung out. He knew what he needed to get the nerve up to hit one of those programs for a job. He needed a nice, sweet dose in the morning, to get his head just right.

In the middle of all this, his grandmother told him that she was taking the younger kids and his mother back to Puerto Rico. They had relatives there, some of whom had money. It would be a better life for the kids, and maybe his mother would get better there, though Georgie couldn't see how.

Georgie couldn't see what difference it would make, since he was rarely home anyway. Then it dawned on him: where was he going to live? No money, and no hope for any, and now they were going to leave him without a bed to sleep in. The thought of actually having to care for himself scared him to death.

Instead, his grandmother offered to turn the apartment over to Georgie and his older brother, Eddie. Even as kids, Eddie and Georgie had had little to do with each other. Eddie was five years older than Georgie, and he had always been a serious and brooding type, given to fits of anger at Georgie's nonstop party style of life. He had left home to go to school in New Jersey; now he was finished and had a job downtown as a computer analyst in a bank.

The family left, with little ceremony, and, right away, Eddie started telling Georgie what to do. "I ain't paying your way forever, stud," he would say, "like your damnfool grandmother. School or work, I don't care. But you party on your own time from now on, you hear!" And Georgie would say nothing. What he wanted to do was tell him he was strung out, tripped out on a broken roller coaster, and that he needed help in a hurry. Eddie was downtown smart; he knew his way around beyond the Bronx; he would know where to get him the help he needed. But to Georgie he might as well have been a stranger; he hardly knew him at all, and what he knew he either hated or feared. So he said nothing, and the hate between them grew.

They rarely saw each other. Eddie was gone all day, working; Georgie was out all night, trying to cop. When they saw each other, they fought constantly, or, rather, Eddie fought with Georgie. The fights had a nightmarish quality to them. The morning hours at home Georgie spent nodding on his bed, riding out the final minutes of a high, or resting from the exhaustion of a night's tramping through the streets. Eddie would walk into the room and shake him, and, through his half-opened eyes, he would peer into the dim light in the bedroom and try to focus on his brother, pacing angrily, back and forth, pointing his finger or his fist. Georgie would try to concentrate on his voice, try to make out what he was saying, but usually he couldn't understand a word. That only made Eddie madder, and he would stalk out, still screaming, threatening to kill him if he found him still in bed when he came home that night.

He took to taking long walks in the afternoons. He liked to follow the snakelike path of Tremont Avenue as it moved here and there and cut through the hardrock cliffs of the Bronx. Sometimes he would go to the pool hall under the el at Jerome Avenue and shoot a little eight ball. Playing pool always relaxed him and made him feel good, reminding him of past summers when his hours passed so much more effortlessly. He would watch the big money games and wish that he was good enough to hustle for his dope money. He would sometimes sit for hours, listening to the sound of the balls as they rolled softly on the felt table and then fell with a resounding thunk into the pockets. He watched the eyes of the players: the studied boredom of the hustlers; the too-bright eyes of shooters playing for money they couldn't afford to lose. He sat there, wordlessly watching, and no one seemed to notice.

Sometimes Georgie would wander into the

movie house just down the street from the pool hall. He would sit in the balcony and watch the movies as if he were in front of a television set, his mind tuning in and out. Often the plots were so broken in his mind that it seemed as if he were seeing four, five and six movies at the same time. He would listen for the sound of the el trains rattling by, lending an eerie quality of broken reality to what was happening on the screen. He wondered how people in movie theaters could be quiet for so long and why they rarely spoke to one another. And he remembered the Hawks and how their screams used to bounce crazily off the high ceiling and fluted walls of the theater; the place seemed so sadly quiet now. And then he would walk out, feeling so much older than he had the day before.

He would walk west, past decrepit apartment buildings, past battered bridge tables and men in T shirts, playing poker, whist and dominoes; past roller skaters and stickball players; on past University Avenue, to the west side of the Bronx, where rents were higher and the streets were emptier and the buildings were made of pink brick and thick glass. He walked on until he reached the river, which he viewed from behind a rusty iron fence on a sheer cliff. Below him, tiny cars were inching north and away from the city, and he thought of long ago in Harlem and how he had loved to watch the cars and trucks head the other way, into the heart of the city. Now there was nothing to look at except the dirty river, which looked as if it had stopped flowing, and a cement plant embedded on its banks.

As the sun dropped before his eyes, he would think of what to do next. It was a long walk home. He usually decided to walk back to University and grab the Tremont bus. It was late, and he was tired. Maybe . . .

Maybe a little head would make him feel better.

•

The summer came, and Georgie was almost seventeen, and he had stopped fooling himself.

He was stealing from his brother as often as possible now. He would wait behind ashcans in an alleyway and watch for his brother to leave in the morning. He would watch him walk down the street and turn the corner, and then he would wait some more, until he was sure he wasn't coming back. Then he would run into the building and up the stairs, and rush inside the apartment. He would empty the drawers, the closets, and his brother's pockets, and search under the bed, behind the toilet, in the medicine cabinet, in the kitchen cupboards. On the floor by the door, he would make a little pile of anything he found that he thought he could sell: new shirts and pants, shoes, tie clips and cuff links, a cigarette lighter. Spare change and an occasional bill went into his pocket. Strange pills that he sometimes found went with him, too; pills were always valuable, if only to rip off another junkie.

He was never satisfied with what he found. Once he found a checkbook and tore out a couple of checks, which he later sold on the street for five dollars. He was afraid to try to cash them himself. He threw the rest of the book out in a rage, frustrated by his being too chickenshit to do anything with it. Exhausted, he would finish his frenzied search by emptying the refrigerator and eating whatever he could find. Then he would head for the bed and nod out, carefully setting an alarm clock to prevent his sleeping beyond the time his brother came home from work. He waited for a long time before he finally sold the clock; after that, he woke up in time on instinct alone.

Once on the street, he headed for Crotona Park to hit the junkie grapevine for nightly tips. Who was holding? What kind of stuff did he have, heavy or cut hard? Was it cheap? Would he give credit? Was anybody back from 'Nam with Asia dust? Were there any easy marks around? Who had just cashed a paycheck? A welfare check? A numbers payoff?

They gathered in the park, the junkie lepers, and whispered their secrets to one another. They had to get the edge. Everything had to be simple, quick, and neat, because, above all, a bust had to be avoided. Copping dope on Riker's Island meant taking somebody's cock up the ass at night and slaving for that somebody during the day. In the early evening, they would gather like ants on a rotting hill and plan for the night's score, then scatter into the darkness.

As long as it was Eddie he was ripping off, Georgie had it easy; he was certain that, despite all his hard talk, Eddie would never put the heat on him. But each week, he was getting less and less for what he was stealing; worse yet, Eddie was being more careful about what he left around. Georgie used to wonder about what was going through the poor bastard's head. It must be driving him crazy, he thought, not being able to leave a damn thing around in his own house. And he knew he was much too quick for Eddie to catch him. After a while, though, he stopped thinking about it. He was happy to have a steady, safe target.

His earlier street training served him well. He slept on rooftops and on subway platforms, or, sometimes, in the bushes in the park, where patrol car headlights rarely penetrated. He was a shadow that was never seen, except when he wanted to be. He practiced his climbing; he sharpened his knowledge of the rooftop highways and backdoor alleyways, preparing for the time when Eddie would not be enough of a source for income, and he would have to start ripping off others at random.

After he copped, he would take his needle kit to one of his rooftop spots, get the needle load ready, and pop it home. He would ride out the first wave up there on the roof, the pink and orange lights of the city below reflecting off the clouds and into his eyes. Sometimes he would nod out for a while, waking to find his cheek sticky from the soft black tar sheets. Then he would walk back to the park to rejoin all the others.

They would sit there into the night, building up one another with street talk of the cosmic high. They traded home remedies for hepatitis and skin sores and crashing. They whispered rumors of new highs, of methadone and mescaline, acid and quaaludes, and of old ones that were making comebacks, like bennies and Coke. There was talk of mixing the drugs: of how downs could cushion the crash back to consciousness after a long nod; of how speed accelerated time and cut down the urge to do a needle; of how methadone had a nice jolt to it, good as skag, and cheaper. And finally, an essential piece of news: Who OD'd, and where did he buy? An OD meant someone was selling some dynamite dust.

In the park, Georgie met Sondra. She was wiry and angular, with a strong face and eyes whose intensity could not be completely washed away by the dope mist. She was just someone to talk to, quiet, in her way, and a little aloof from the rest, as if she knew all about the lies that passed between them in the patchy grass. One night, sitting there next to her, Georgie was jolted by an overwhelming rush, the last remnant of an earlier fix, and she cradled his head in her hands and let him ride it out against her, her heartbeat in his ear giving him something steady to hold on to. He saw her differently, after that.

Gradually, the two of them parted from the rest and hunted on the hot concrete together. Huddling on rooftops, they made their plans together, she in a fading sweater and torn jeans, he in a T shirt and tight black pants. They shivered in the sometimes chilly September wind. She wouldn't let him get a gun. He wouldn't let her hustle for twenty bucks on the street corners. They lived from day to day on petty thievery, pausing only to clutch at each other for a few hours in Georgie's bed when Eddie was out of the house.

He learned, after a while, that she saw the junkie life as only temporary, that, though she loved him, she would leave him in a minute if she lost hope that the two of them would not somehow come out on the other side together. There was a toughness in her that drew him toward her, but frightened him just the same. She handled what money they had with a cold efficiency and kept both of them going on a steady diet of stolen fruit, Hostess Twinkies, and milk. He found himself depending on her for the final decisions: she was more careful and less impulsive than he, and she kept them out of situations that might lead to violence, or, worse, to a bust.

It was early winter when Sondra found out she was pregnant. She said nothing to Georgie until the weather got really cold, and sleeping on rooftops or in the bushes became impractical. She hadn't told him before then, perhaps because she was wondering what she should do. She was a junkie, and an abortion would be a lot better than a junkie baby, bred to the needle from birth; but she was also a Latin Catholic, and child-murder was, in her mind, still the worst crime imaginable. She waited until she had no choice, and then she told him.

His first reaction was all bravado, as she expected. They would get married. He would find a job, a good one. Maybe they could go to Puerto Rico. His relatives could find them a house, a nice one, by the water. The baby would change everything. Even as his stupidity angered her, she had to smile.

Then, of course, he thought some more about it and took to brooding. He was cold toward her, even nasty. The change in him was enough for her to make up her mind. She woke him one afternoon, in the apartment, and told him what she was going to do.

"I'm going away, Georgie. I'm going to kick. I can't do this to the baby. You can stay, or you can come. It's all the same to me." And she left him, and went uptown, to a clinic for junkies on 231st Street.

For a couple of weeks, Georgie pretended to himself that she would be back, that she would stay away for only a short while. How, he thought, could she provide for the baby without a man? He forgot that she had done most of the providing before. When the weeks turned into months, her absence began to torture him. He needed her not only because he loved her, but also because he was finding it more and more difficult to sustain his life and his habit on the street from day to day. She was the cement in his life, and, without her, he began to fall apart. He went for days without eating, until, in a frenzy, he broke a window and grabbed an armful of cans from a supermarket. He could hear the store alarm ripping through his head as he raced down the street, the cans spilling from his trembling arms. He lived on warm and sickly sweet peaches and pale green peas for a whole week after that.

He got more and more frantic about copping dope. Whenever he made a substantial buy, it was all he could do to keep from shooting it all. He knew that what he should do was limit himself to a steady dose and maintain it. It was the only way to survive without the needle becoming murderously demanding. But the more frightened he got, the farther off he wanted to fly, and the doses he needed to get there grew larger in leaps and bounds. He awoke on a cold December morning and found himself lying along the ledge of a building, six stories up, humping it almost, with one leg over the side. He almost fell off in his fear.

He was afraid to go home now, because he was sure his brother would find him. He found it hard to keep track of time. Nights and days no longer stood out in his mind. The faces he saw on the streets all looked the same. Their eyes looked through him, as if he weren't there.

In January, after a week spent shivering in hallways, choking on the urine smell in the air, he went home. All he wanted was to lie down on his bed and sleep, sleep forever. He stopped caring about his brother, or what he might do if he found him there. He climbed the steps slowly; he was barely strong enough to make it. He had a hacking cough, and his chest ached with each breath he took as he climbed. His whole face was wet with slime and unbearably itchy. His hand trembled as he slipped the key into the lock.

The key wouldn't turn. He almost cried. He tried again, and again, and then he started kicking the door. It opened, and a woman he had never seen before looked out at him angrily.

"What the hell you doin' out here, boy? You a goddamn junkie! Get the hell out of here, before I call a cop. Go on, get out of here." She was bigger than he was, and she pushed him away from the doorway easily.

"My brother," he whispered hoarsely. "My brother . . ."

"Junkies ain't got no brothers. Now get your ugly

face out of here before I let the dope out of you with a butcher knife." And she turned and went inside. He staggered down the stairs and went away.

A couple of days later, Georgie was rousted along with a half dozen others in a routine vagrancy bust at Crotona Park. He had nothing on him that they could bust him for, though they might have hassled him over the needle marks on his arms and legs. But this was just a routine harassment bust, and the bored cops at the station house weren't interested in three hours of paperwork over a bunch of half-dead bodies they had dragged into the patrol cars. They were content with just getting the bunch off the streets for a night.

After about twenty minutes at the precinct, Georgie walked up to the sergeant at the booking desk.

"Sit down, kid, we'll get to you," the cop said.

"I want to tell you something," Georgie said.

"Well, say it and sit down."

"I'm a dope fiend," he said. "I want to turn myself in."

In the summer of 1966, the residents of most of the nation's black ghettos collectively made the jump from reform to revolt, from resentment to hatred. From city to city, they began to burn down, street by street, the buildings that were their homes. They threw rocks at whites in passing cars. They shot at policemen. They threw firebombs at fire trucks. They looted the cheap, overpriced department stores and furniture "warehouses" that, through rigged contracts and credit agreements, had looted them for years. It was, for most whites, a frightening spectacle.

New York City, which contains not one but two of the country's largest and most desolate black ghettos, was rather mysteriously spared that ordeal. The city had a new mayor that summer, a young liberal Republican named John Lindsay, who extracted enough political ammunition from his Kennedy-like

persona and his own considerable talents to over-
throw an entrenched and tired Democratic machine. His promises of reform later bore bitter fruit
for many city residents (and for his own political career), but during the first few months of his administration, the city politic exuded a feeling that in it was
captured at least a small remnant of the buried
Camelot.

To keep in touch with the volatile metabolism of
the ghetto streets, Lindsay employed an informal
team of young City Hall aides. They were really
more like political advance men: all bright and ath-
letic, with a quality of New York *chutzpah* about
them. They wore no ties and jackets while working,
preferring instead sweat shirts and chinos and wind-
breakers with "The Mayor's Office" printed on the
back. It was not unusual for them to establish contact
with young community leaders by playing a few
games of half-court basketball.

All during that first hot summer, the Lindsay
team fanned out into the city streets and made their
contacts on playground pavements or while leaning
on cars wet with water from an open fire hydrant. By
circumventing black and white bureaucracies and
political protocol, they were able to gauge accurately
which situations were truly dangerous and which
weren't, thus allowing the Mayor the luxury of knowing where to concentrate his attention. That summer, the six o'clock and eleven o'clock TV news
shows would run several newsreels of Lindsay in
shirt sleeves, walking the streets of Harlem or
Bedford-Stuyvesant, talking with residents, shaking

hands, answering flashy but blunt questions from some street youngblood. Sometimes, in the foreground, the camera would show the Mayor's young aides forming a wedge through the crowd for the Mayor to follow.

One of the members of this little Lindsay gang was a young black Morgan State graduate named Ted Gross. As one of the few blacks in the Lindsay inner circle, Gross rose very quickly. He began as a mayoral assistant, assigned to work in the area of minority problems. His salary was $17,500, hardly enough to pay for his wardrobe, if his public appearance was any indication of his taste in clothing. Fur coats in winter and flashy linen suits in summer were essential to the Gross look. Nonetheless, according to Sid Davidoff, then one of Lindsay's top young aides, "Teddy was good in the neighborhoods." In the summer of 1968, a Housing Authority policeman killed a Brooklyn youth whom he saw running from the scene of a burglary. Police reports indicated that there wasn't likely to be any trouble from neighborhood residents over the incident, but the Lindsay team sent out Gross to check, just in case. Sure enough, Gross reported, the area was a potential firestorm. Based on the Gross report, Lindsay decided to make a personal trip there to cool things down. The trip was a success, and the Mayor personally thanked Gross for averting a possible riot.

In August of 1970, Gross was appointed Deputy Commissioner of the Youth Services Administration. YSA was a branch of the huge Human Resources Administration superagency, whose rubric included welfare programs and all other social services. YSA's function was to oversee all the city's youth programs, from hopscotch tournaments to job programs. When Gross was assigned to YSA, the agency was just beginning to cope with the sudden outbreak of street-gang violence in the South Bronx. The agency was rapidly becoming the central dumping ground for the street-gang problem. Police department officials were anxious for YSA to take some of the pressure of containing the gangs away from their already overworked staffs. Understandably, police officials were fearful that some young cop half crazy with nerves and exhaustion would blow away a couple of gang members and inflame an entire neighborhood. Community people were complaining that South Bronx gang leaders had insinuated themselves into YSA programs and had in some cases co-opted YSA storefronts for their own gang headquarters. The gang leaders were complaining either that YSA had no job programs for gang members, or that YSA street workers favored some gangs over others.

It was obvious that Ted Gross was chosen for the YSA post because of his previous street experience. If anyone could deal with gang leaders, the Lindsay people reasoned, Gross could. "He knows the city and its young people," said the Mayor himself on making the appointment. His salary jumped to $26,400; he was a young man on the move.

The Gross strategy for attacking the gang problem was simple; borrowing from his days on the Lindsay advance team, he established a cadre of street workers to serve as liaisons with the gangs. In choosing his workers, he was careful to select people he knew were wired to the street grapevine, and not those who had just curried political favor. Within six months, his intelligence on street-gang activity surpassed the police department's; his people knew who was crazy and who wasn't; who could be trusted and who should be feared. In short, Gross attained the same administrative luxury that the advance team had given the Mayor: the knowledge of where to direct his priorities. His work with the street gangs earned him a promotion to Commissioner of YSA eleven months after he had joined the agency. In less than a year and a half as a city official, Gross's salary had been raised to $35,000 a year.

But something must have happened along the way. Maybe some of his older uptown contacts began calling on old political debts. Or maybe it was just that, with his expensive tastes, even $35,000 a year wasn't a hell of a lot of money. Or maybe the frustrations of being the house black with the finger in the dike got to be too much for him. But not long after he became Commissioner, there was a subtle shift in his style—from substance to slick, from street-wise young politico to full-time hustler.

It was almost as if Gross were trying to prove that he hadn't sold out to the white establishment. Suddenly, he was using his driver and city limousine wherever he went. He started spending money freely on everything and everybody. Even some of his inside staffers began to wonder where he was getting the money for some of the things he was buying.

He also developed an air of phony macho that hardly resembled the Ted Gross who was so effective during a hot summer five years before. He became fond of tough, oblique little outbursts when he discussed business with his staff before any outsiders. Once, while he was in his office discussing the street-gang problem with a reporter, an aide came in with some papers. The aide told Gross that he had checked with the police, and they had nothing to report on the theft of some photographic and stereo equipment from the trunk of Gross's limousine the night before. "Don't worry about it, I'll take care of it," he said. The reporter, curious as to what Gross could do that the police could not, asked how he was going to "take care of it." "Oh, I'll just go back uptown to where I was last night. Then I'll find me the first nigger junkie on the block, and I'll beat his ass until he tells me who did the job."

Before someone high up could take notice of Gross's spending habits, he ran into trouble with his gang crisis squad and with some of the street gangs themselves. In the winter of 1971, the Bronx crisis squad was hoping to set up a program in the South Bronx which would supply some of the toughest Bronx gangs with storefront clubhouses if they cooperated in neighborhood YSA programs. Gross had tentatively agreed to go to bat for the program with Lindsay himself. Even so, the chances for approval were pretty slim; the idea of legitimizing street gangs by publicly funding them was a bit too politically hot for City Hall.

Squad members were already upset with Gross.

One of their members was Eddie Vincente, a twenty-seven-year-old veteran of the fifties' Bronx street gangs. Eddie was probably the most effective member of the squad; he was all street and had little trouble in winning the respect of gang leaders. After some early success in preventing intergang wars from erupting over rumors or minor incidents, Eddie began working on the grandiose notion of getting every major gang in the Bronx to sign an intergang treaty and alliance. This giant alliance would be called "The Family," and every gang would become a single division in the larger gang. The idea had just enough vision in it for gang leaders to be interested in its possibilities. And Spanish Eddie, as he was called, felt that once unified under a single name, the gangs could do virtually anything, if someone provided them with the right kind of social vision. Even the police admitted to as many as ten thousand gang members in the Bronx alone.

In the midst of the project, Spanish Eddie and ten other crisis squad members were suddenly transferred from the Bronx to Brooklyn. Even so, Spanish Eddie continued to work on the Brotherhood Family in his spare time. When Eddie was shot trying to prevent a gun battle in the West Farms area, crisis squad members blamed it on Gross. Gross must have considered Vincente's idea far too dangerous, but rather than just veto it, they felt, he had abruptly transferred him. Outraged, Eddie had simply pushed harder for his dream; taking foolish chances, he was nearly killed.

Spring came, and there was still no decision on

the storefronts from Gross. However, word came to the crisis squad from city bureaucracy sources that Lindsay would be willing to allow some money for the project if the money was not specifically allocated for the street gangs' use. So some crisis squad members went ahead and assured their gangs that the storefronts were a real possibility.

But the money for them never materialized. And the gang leaders turned on YSA squad members. Alliances between gangs that had taken months to arrange fell apart overnight. Squad members were forbidden to walk on turf where they did most of their street work. Those gangs who were still friendly toward the YSA people were furious with Gross.

One of Gross's Bronx friends owned a bowling alley in the Bronx, and Gross was seen there quite often. Gang members who had seen him come and go in his limousine and expensive clothing were openly resentful over not getting the money they wanted while Gross was living, they said, like a high-class pimp. One gang member swears there was a five-hundred-dollar contract put out on Gross. He also remembers a night when a hundred or so gang members surrounded the bowling alley that Gross frequented, ready to kill him or hold him for ransom. He says, somewhat ruefully, that Gross managed to sneak out.

Squad leaders and gang members had good reason for being angry with Gross. Most of their money was apparently going into his pocket. Early in the summer of 1972, Gross was called back to New York from his vacation to explain some mysterious expenses and questionable contracts that had turned up in a Controller's audit of YSA's books. Gross was unable to explain the discrepancies. In the fall, the city's investigations unit expanded the Beame audit and found that Gross was involved in more than just some personal expenditures of city money.

Almost from the day he began his tenure as Commissioner, he was taking kickbacks from potential YSA contractors, starting with a pair of airline tickets to Hawaii and peaking with a twenty-one-thousand-dollar payment on a two-hundred-thousand-dollar-plus YSA contract. He set up some friends with a dummy foundation, and then contracted work to that foundation; he also leased eight cars for the foundation that were used mostly by his own executives. He threw huge parties for friends and staffers at different restaurants around the city, spending as much as five hundred dollars at once. He manipulated the agency's petty cash fund to arrange loans for himself and other YSA members. One three-hundred-dollar expenditure was listed as for a ball game. He also junketed down to Puerto Rico with six others on city money. In October of 1972, Gross was forced to resign from his commissionership; four months later, he was indicted on eight counts of having accepted kickbacks. The indictment stated that he had accepted his first kickback a few days after becoming Commissioner; his last one came the day he sent Mayor Lindsay his resignation. Eventually he pleaded guilty to two of the counts and was sentenced to three years in jail.

Spanish Eddie Vincente left the city around the

same time Gross left for prison. His was, in many ways, a much sadder story than the Gross story. Though his scheme for allying the street gangs sounded more than a little idealistic, he had, before he was reassigned, signed on sixty-eight gangs to his treaty. He had also attracted the attention of black underworld figures, who worried about losing those street gangs they used as cheap labor. Older, larger gangs who saw Vincente's plan as a threat to well-established protection territories were also concerned with his success in signing new gangs. So unprovoked wars were begun with brotherhood gangs. Gang members still remember silent squadrons of Savage Skulls openly strutting down Vyse Avenue to challenge the Peacemakers, an early brotherhood gang. Members wearing brotherhood gang colors were shot from moving cars, were stabbed in movie theaters, were pushed in front of buses. Phony confrontations were arranged, where brotherhood gangs were lured into a show of force at a given time and a given geographic location, only to have the police suddenly turn up in large numbers, tipped by an anonymous phone call. The rippling effect of hostile intergang relations spread to gangs throughout the brotherhood, and the treaty began to fall apart. The fact that the gang fever had spread north to the Bronx borders, and that there were now as many as eighty-five to a hundred different gangs in the Bronx alone, didn't help matters any. A single incident between the Black Spades and Intercrime up on Baychester Boulevard could eventually provoke a seven-gang war down on Southern Boulevard. It was not really surprising when Vincente was shot in the face trying to stop a gang fight. Confined to his apartment after his release from the hospital, Eddie had to resign his job at YSA. Eventually, he left the city and moved upstate.

Ironically, the gang leaders made one last attempt to rescue the brotherhood family. Shocked by the shooting of Spanish Eddie, gang leaders called for a massive meeting in the South Bronx between all gang presidents and war counselors. Leaders of more than seventy gangs came to a high school gym prepared to hammer out some sort of borough-wide peace treaty in honor of Spanish Eddie. It was an event: vows of brotherhood being exchanged between seventeen-year-olds who had last seen one another peering out from behind the fenders of parked cars, their hands sweating on the barrels of pistols and rifles.

But with the coming of summer, the melodrama of the big meeting was only a memory, and Spanish Eddie was just another guy who had been shot on the street. Gang members got back to what they knew how to do best: vent their energies in petty and destructive wars among themselves. The meeting did serve one purpose, though. It was taped in its entirety by the police department, and it later became the source both for several future indictments against gang leaders, and for many of the more than four thousand gang dossiers that the Bronx Street Gang Task Force has on file today.

After turning himself in, Georgie was shuffled from one office to another. He spent his nights in small detention cells in different court buildings and police precincts, by himself, mostly, since they were rarely used for overnighters. He was grateful for the privacy, grateful for the powdery food, and most grateful for the stifling steam heat that poured through the pipes in the thick stone buildings.

He was taken to see all sorts of people. A police community relations officer. A Family Court judge. A probation officer. A Legal Aid lawyer. A psychiatric social worker. He went along with their probing reluctantly, answering all the questions with replies he felt obvious. Did he have a family? No. Had he been shooting dope for long? No. Was he going to school at all? No. Had he committed any crimes? Yes.

They questioned him closely about how he supported his habit. They asked him if he knew certain

people. He knew none of the people they asked
about. They asked him where he was on such and
such a date, and he said, most of the time, that he
couldn't remember. They finally asked him, point
blank, if he had ever shot or stabbed anyone. No, he
answered flatly. Had he used a gun in any of his
robberies? No.

He felt very foggy and a little numb as he wandered from cluttered office to cubbyhole and back
again. The social worker put him through a whole
series of questions that seemed completely weird. He
had trouble answering many of them. The lawyer
was even stranger. He tried to convince Georgie that
he was a sick person. Every time he asked Georgie
a question, he would answer it himself. Dazed as he
was, he almost told the guy to fuck off. I'm no psycho,
he thought to himself.

He kept waiting for some kind of violent withdrawal attack, but none came. A police doctor exam-
ined him shortly after he turned himself in. He
remembered that a little better than all the other
things. The guy had handled him as if he were a
collection of automobile parts hanging up on a rack.
He told Georgie he was developing a case of pneu-
monia and gave him heavy dosages of antibiotics for
it. Maybe it was the pills that helped him do without
dope.

He would have been content to spend his days
going from office to office and answering a few questions, if that were all it took to guarantee him a warm
bed and supper at night. He didn't care much about
anything else. After ten days or so, he found himself

on a dark green prison bus, with narrow slits in the back and tiny barred windows, headed for an upstate prison called Woodburn. There were others on the bus, but Georgie ignored them. He shivered in the unheated bus and, hunched in the corner, fell asleep. The last thing he thought of was that seventeen was his worst year.

Woodburn was a minimum security prison for first offenders. A lot of kids between sixteen and eighteen got sent there after their first bust, unless they already had a long history of juvenile-delinquency arrests. Georgie spent four months there and did very little, except to emerge slowly from his comatose state and become more aware of who he was again, and where he was. Woodburn was mostly a royal pain. He had to mop floors. He had to go to classes, to try to learn how to read again. He had to wash dishes at night. The beds were hard, the food bad.

Junkies were at the bottom at Woodburn, and Georgie learned fast not to hang with them. Those who were sent up on ordinary criminal charges, like robbery or assault, would beat on the junkies unmercifully. Junkies were thrown down the laundry chute. They were thrown naked into the prison cesspool. They were tied to their bedposts and beaten with wet towels. Georgie just stayed by himself and said nothing to anyone. The others thought him crazy and were a little scared of him.

Georgie saw somebody stabbed with a butcher knife while he was at Woodburn. It happened while he was in the kitchen, bringing in the dirty dishes from dinner. He was just putting them down on a countertop when someone ran through the kitchen doors, hesitated for a second right behind him, and then started for one of the cooks, who was standing in the back icing a cake. There must have been a noise, or something, because the cook turned around to see what was happening. Georgie looked up just as the inmate plunged the wide blade into the man's chest. His eyes seemed to fly out of his head, and slowly he raised his hands toward his chest. Then he fell forward hard, his hands still raised in an almost pleading position. He hit the floor, hard, and blood shot out of his mouth and nose all over the floor.

The knife twisted violently as the body hit the floor, and, for a while, the blood poured out in a steady stream. His hands and legs twitched every few seconds. Georgie stood paralyzed, watching the dead man, remembering every detail, until the guards appeared and dragged away the guy who killed the cook. Then they pushed and shoved all the other prisoners who had run in to see what had happened, herding them out of the kitchen and back to their bunks.

Afterward one of the other prisoners told him to say he had seen nothing, because otherwise he would have to serve as a witness in a murder trial and might get tied up with the law long after his sentence was up. When he was asked whether he had seen anything, he said he had been outside in the dining area when it happened. They didn't ask again.

In four months, Georgie was back on the street; dried out, a little healthier, but with no place to stay and no idea of where to start looking. The only place he could think of going was back to Crotona Park. The park had always been home to him. He tried not to think of why he was going back. In prison, they had repeated, over and over again, that an addict can't go back to his old life, can't return to his old crowd, because familiar patterns breed other familiar patterns, and it was an odds-on bet that a junkie would be groping for the needle in the dark once he was surrounded by the same four walls again. He told himself that he was really going there to search for J.J., the one straight friend he figured he could still count on. In the back of his mind, he knew he was fooling himself. He hadn't seen J.J. in more than a year. He might have moved or even gone away to school.

He knew what he was really looking for, as soon as he set down his feet on the familiar concrete of Tremont Avenue. His palms and underarms began to sweat, and his pulse picked up quickly, pounding adrenaline into his brain. He was walking to the spot near the water fountain, where the junkies used to sit in the shadows and plot away their lives. They didn't look up at him until he was almost on them. There was silence; the ones he knew couldn't quite place his face.

"What's happenin', Georgie? You finally crack out of the slams?" somebody finally said, and Georgie smiled weakly back. He settled down on a bench and began listening anxiously.

•

Georgie was barely conscious. The months in jail, away from dope, had dropped his tolerance way down. He tried to compensate for that when he prepared for his first needle. But he was a little drunk from too much wine, and he figured he could take a nice stiff nod, anyway. After the needle went home, he panicked and quickly decided to grab a cup of coffee, just to mute things down a bit. The first jolt hit him as he walked out of the park. He staggered a bit, and his eyes rolled up. Then he walked carefully off the path and into the grass and sat down, resting his chin on his knees.

When he woke up, he was lying in about the same place, and he was sore all over. He got up, grimacing, and tried to look around. He almost fell over, but, instead, staggered back and leaned against a tree. He felt as if the rough bark were cutting into his hand, and he tried to shift his weight a bit. He sat down again and took a deep breath, trying to clear his head. Where could he go now, anyway? he thought. He fell asleep leaning against a tree.

●

A week later, Georgie was picked up with a dime bag of dope in his back pocket while he was harassing people for small change on a street corner. He was back in jail two days after that.

Technically, Georgie had no record yet; this time, though, he was charged with possession and sent up for eight months to a year. He wound up serving the minimum time; one thing he had learned in all his years on the street was how to keep out of trouble when the pressure was on.

During his second stay in prison, two things happened: he met a prisoner named Eddie, and he heard from Sondra again. Eddie was a Puerto Rican with an Indian face who ran his own little clique in Woodburn. Georgie knew him slightly from his first stay, but this time he bunked up in the same section with him. Eddie spoke hardly any English, but Georgie looked like a Latin brother, and Eddie took him in, granting him the protection of running with one of the tougher prison crowds and making his time there a good deal easier. Eddie got out of prison a month before Georgie did, but by then Georgie had status of his own.

Then came the letter from Sondra, and the news that Georgie was the father of a little girl. Her letter was cold and short. All she wanted to do, she said, was to let him know what had happened to his child. It was only right, she said. Still Georgie was left with the feeling that there was more in the letter than that. He decided he would write back.

He wrote her in a tortured scrawl, painfully searching for the right words, tearing up several half-finished letters before he sent one off. He decided to be tough, to let her know where he was, and he wrote demanding to know when he could see the baby, and asking how she was going to be able to take care of it. He almost added that he wanted to marry her, but he held that impulse back. He wasn't sure he was ready for that.

She wrote him back. She wanted to know why

he was in prison. Did he still do dope? How long would he be locked up? She asked these questions bluntly, not disguising the contempt she felt for him. He was discouraged. He almost didn't write back. In a curious way, though, the letter brought back strong memories of Sondra, of when they were together. He sat down and wrote her about what had happened to him in the last year, as best as he could tell it.

They continued to write to each other while he served his time. He got the feeling that she wanted to live with him; that, faced with the choice of moving back in with her mother in disgrace, and losing the child to her in the bargain, or moving in with Georgie, as bad as his future might look, she would rather be with him. But he knew she would never admit that.

The first person he went looking for when he got out was Eddie. Eddie was living over on West Tremont, about a mile west of Georgie's old neighborhood. What he wanted from Eddie was simple: a job and an apartment. He bused over to the area and asked some street-corner dudes about Eddie. They told him he could find him over on Morton Place, a little side street that ran from University to Harrison, one block north of Tremont. He lived, they said, in an apartment building on the corner of Morton and Harrison, but he could usually be found sitting on the stoop outside the building. "You can't miss him," he was told. "He always wears his colors."

Georgie had no idea what colors were. I've been out of touch, he thought. Must be all that time in the hole. He walked a short block and turned the corner on Morton. He could see Eddie from the corner, his shiny, closely cropped blue-black hair weaving and bobbing as he talked to someone. His back was turned, and Georgie could see he was wearing a denim jacket, cut off at the sleeves, with some kind of colored design and fancy lettering on the back. As he got closer, he could make out the design and the letters a little better. There was a bright red skeleton, robed in black, with a red scythe in its hand. Surrounding the design were the words REAPERS BRONX.

There were, he figured, at least a dozen others standing or sitting near Eddie. As he got closer, they all began to look at him. Out of the corner of his eye, he saw a couple of others across the street stand up and stare, and then begin to cross the street toward him. He became aware that there were others walking about twenty feet behind him and closing the gap.

Eddie was still talking, and he didn't look up until Georgie was almost on top of him. By then, Georgie was enclosed within a tight semicircle of about fifteen, casually standing around and leaving Georgie no room to exit.

"Hey, coño, que pasa?" Georgie said, and Eddie looked up at him. Then Eddie smiled broadly and clapped him on the back. The circle of hostile faces dissipated immediately. Eddie sent one of them around the corner to pick up a couple of quart bottles of beer. They sat on the stoop, slugged down the beer, and talked away the afternoon.

Georgie found an apartment on Harrison Avenue, off the corner of Tremont, for Sondra, himself, and the baby. As Bronx apartments went, it wasn't bad; it was sunny, with fairly large rooms; though the halls and stairwells were dark and worn, they were clean. Money was a problem, but, for the time being, Sondra would be collecting welfare payments until, of course, Georgie went out and got a job.

For Georgie, this was the best of all possible worlds. He had hardly expected things to work out so smoothly. Getting the apartment had been no problem; when he got around to mentioning it to Eddie, he told him just to let him know when they would be moving in. He could set the whole thing up with a couple of days' notice. "You as big outside as you were inside," Georgie told him, with a smile.

Getting a job was a different thing, though. Eddie wasn't working, and neither were most of the other jacket-wearers who hung out with him. "You can get a gig around here once in a while," one of the others told him, "but nothing steady." Eddie kept saying not to worry about it, because, as long as he lived in the neighborhood, his people would take care of him. But Georgie was worried about convincing Sondra. Should he lie? Tell her he had a job? He stayed at Eddie's apartment for a couple of days and thought about what to do. She knew he was out of prison by then, and she would be waiting to hear from him.

On a Saturday morning, he grabbed the Jerome Avenue train and headed for the clinic where Sondra and the baby were staying. He walked into the clinic, which was located in an old house, and stopped in the hallway, blocked by a huge desk. Behind the desk sat a hard-looking black dude with a phone and a clipboard in front of him.

"Who you here to see, man?" the guy asked him, smiling, but only with his mouth. He told him who.

The dude picked up the phone. Then he looked up and smiled again, a little more broadly. "You Georgie?" he asked.

Georgie nodded and smiled back. Another guy came down the stairs and told Georgie to follow him. He walked up a couple of steep flights of stairs, and then past several rooms decorated with posters and paintings, and into a large white room with several beds. She was sitting on one of the beds, holding an infant uncomfortably in her arms.

He sat down, looked at her, and said hello. She didn't look happy, or even surprised, to see him. He kept telling himself that she was sizing him up, in that careful way of hers, but he was more than a little hurt by her lack of warmth. His guide left them, and they sat looking at each other, wordlessly.

"She's cute," Georgie finally said, and tentatively poked a finger at the baby's middle. The baby gurgled and kicked around a bit, but Sondra said nothing. He noticed that she had gained weight, not much, but enough to make her look healthier. Her face looked older and tired, very tired. Why won't she say anything to me? he thought.

"You look good, Georgie," she finally said, quietly, and Georgie thought about it. He felt better, physically anyway. Now that she mentioned it, he felt better than he could remember feeling in a long time. The needle sores that had pockmarked his arms and legs were healing, and he had also gained some weight.

"You do, too, Sondra," he answered, embarrassed. Then, as an afterthought: "I don't do dope anymore." It was true; he hadn't thought about doing dope in months.

She smiled a little at that and hugged the baby. Then he smiled, too, and touched her hand. She looked at him.

"I got us a place. We can move in whenever we want to." He hesitated. "I don't have a job, yet. I got to keep looking, though." She seemed to pause and think about that. He sucked in a breath, and waited.

"I can move out of here anytime, Georgie," she finally said. "Just let me know when."

In New York City, organized crime has traditionally been an employer for members of excluded ethnic and racial groups. It has offered a way of sneaking around and through middle class fortress walls and stealing a little economic and political clout for the next generation to build on. The Irish did it; so did the Italians and the Jews; now blacks and Hispanics are doing the same. There are no job requirements, no diplomas, no exams; applicants are judged solely on the basis of their talents and their potential use to the organization. The pay is much better then anywhere else; there is room for advancement, and, though anticompetitive practices tend to be tough, new businesses can thrive and succeed. Like the bumper sticker says, the Mafia is an equal opportunity employer.

Likewise, street gangs have always been a kind of minor league for a career in professional crime.

For one thing, the longer a kid has been out on the streets, the less likely he will ever be able to earn a decent wage working at so-called legitimate jobs. Take the average gang member; he is a school dropout with, chances are, at least a small arrest record. He is probably functionally illiterate; his skills, if he has any, are undeveloped; his record limits him to an unskilled job at the minimum wage. Many gang members can't qualify for Youth Corps summer jobs as clerks: they can't even write their own names. None of this is a hindrance, as far as local crime bosses are concerned, if the kid can handle a gun and has a taste for brutality. Even drug addiction isn't a total liability; if a junkie has a skill that will prove valuable for one reason or another, a pusher may pay him in dope and receive as an extra dividend a loyalty bordering on the fanatic.

This is not to say that sadism or ruthlessness is the only valuable skill in organized crime. Malcolm X wrote in his autobiography of Archie, the numbers man, who had no high school education but was able to keep complicated numbers accounts completely in his head, thus never leaving a trace of evidence behind. It was not unusual for crime organizations to tap resources of talent that schools had overlooked or ignored. While conventional employers locked their doors to the street dropout, organized crime recruited from the same huge untapped pool of talent.

By the time the latest wave of street gangs reached its peak, the structure of organized crime in New York had undergone an enormous change. Once totally dominated by five well-knit Mafia families, such profitable ventures as heroin and cocaine, prostitution, the numbers, and even loan sharking had come under the control of local black and Latin bosses. At first the five families had encouraged the growth of local captains who ran virtually autonomous operations and paid out a flat percentage of the profit to the organization. Black and Latin neighborhoods were proving increasingly difficult for white overlords to handle; by hiring blacks and Latins to oversee such operations, the risk was minimized and the profit maximized. Also, the postwar economic boom was rapidly producing a more substantial white middle class; Italians, Irish, and Jews were able to leave ghetto areas in increased numbers, to be replaced mainly by blacks and Puerto Ricans. Since the ghetto was the prime market for organized crime's big moneymakers—gambling, prostitution, and drugs—the Mafia found it necessary to deal more and more with blacks and Latins.

Then many of the local black and Latin captains became powerful in their own right, powerful enough to challenge the dominance of the old Mafia capos. No less a figure than Joey Gallo foresaw just such a happening. Serving a lengthy sentence in prison, he left convinced that an alliance between a family gang and local black kingpins could dethrone the aging families and dominate the criminal network of the whole city. Gallo died as a victim of the struggle that ensued when he tried to implement his plan. The result was that whole areas of huge profit potential fell into the hands of tough black and Latin independents. Spanish Raymond, the cocaine kingpin, is said to gross twenty million dollars a year in his operation alone.

The two most prolific sources for the manpower necessary to build local criminal empires were the streets and the prisons. Temporary prisons like the Tombs or Riker's Island brought together large numbers of ghetto youths from virtually identical backgrounds but different geographical locations. This meant that sixteen-year-olds who had never ventured from within a ten-block radius of a single Bronx neighborhood except on an occasional group excursion were suddenly making contacts all over the city. Such contacts were later valuable in structuring street gangs, for they often determined where a prisoner, once released, might decide to make his new home. Older, more experienced prisoners had usually served time at a larger state institution. They were to serve both as future gang leaders and as pipelines to black and Latin mobs all over the city.

Gangs like the Savage Skulls had codes constructed to resemble the complex laws of a crime mob. Initiations often sent new members to the hospital; sometimes they were even fatal. Even a member of a junior division of a gang would be severely tested before being admitted to regular gang membership. In 1972, when the president of a Young Skull chapter demanded membership in a regular Skull division, Skull leaders were enraged at his gall. He was invited to a Skull meeting and told that, in his case, initiation would be bypassed, since they already knew just how bad he was. On his way out, two Skulls jumped him in the hall and beat him with lead pipes, fracturing his skull. After a month in the hospital, he came out and rejoined the gang.

A Skull member couldn't just decide one day that he wanted out of the gang, either. The Skulls were involved in too many activities that police wanted to know more about; so a Skull membership was a lifetime deal. James Puig, a Skulls vice president, decided to leave the gang in 1972; soon after, he was found shot to death on an empty street, with four bullets in his chest. Eventually, a dozen Skulls were arrested for the murder.

That kind of discipline was ideal for preparing a gang member for a career in organized crime, and an enterprising gang leader who grew bored with the small-time life of the street gang found it easy to find more exciting and lucrative work with a local black or Latin mob. But mob leaders found it infinitely cheaper simply to purchase a local gang's services outright. The ease with which this was accomplished varied with the degree to which a street gang was already involved in criminal activity. If a gang was simply a formalized local clique, as were most local Bronx gangs, and if petty thievery was the most serious form of crime they regularly indulged in, it might be easy to win them over by selling them handguns and fancy knives at a cut-rate price. Even a relatively benign street gang longed for an arsenal of some kind, as a means of gaining status in the street hierarchy. Such a gang, suddenly heavily armed, would inevitably get involved in some sort of problem either with another gang or with the police. The trick, then, was to move in with offers of armed support in the event of a gang war, or with legal help if a gang leader faced a serious arrest problem. Thus heavily indebted, the gang could then be utilized as free runners for drug drops or gambling slips.

A gang that was already heavily involved in thefts and protection rackets posed another kind of problem. For one, they focused police attention on a particular area, which meant potential trouble for anyone else operating in the same area. Secondly, such a gang offered the kind of crude, unpredictable competition that a well-organized mob boss could ill afford. Members of such gangs were used to taking chances that the organized mobs recognized as stupid and expensive; they were also much quicker on the trigger, and could do a lot of damage if not dealt with quickly and efficiently. A mutually profitable partnership would be proposed, which could result in a street gang obtaining a small territory to exploit as they saw fit, in return for performing such tasks as might otherwise prove too risky for mob members. Such tasks often included contracts on the life of a troublesome pusher or an ambitious local independent, often for as little as fifty or seventy-five dollars. There was little risk involved for anybody in such murders, because gang presidents would simply subcontract them to young gang members eager to win status and acceptance in the gang. If he was caught, it didn't really matter; since he was underage, he would get off with easy time in a juvenile institution.

In 1972, two Bronx mobsters were on the verge of warring with each other over drug territory in the Southeast Bronx. Both recognized the costs involved in such a war; both were too greedy and stubborn to compromise and split the territory between them. So they simply subcontracted the entire war. One mob hired the Black Spades; the other hired the Secret and Imperial Bachelors. The shooting reached the point where seven kids were gunned down within thirty-six hours, though only one died. All were lined up execution style against building walls and shot with high caliber rifles. None was older than seventeen. Within a few months, Bachelor and Spade divisions all over the Bronx were at war with one another. Other gangs became involved as the violence inevitably spilled over. Both the Spades and the Bachelors refused any claims of neutrality by stray members from other gangs who accidentally stumbled on a combat zone. That war brought the total 1972 figure for deaths due to street-gang activity to the highest level yet recorded.

From the start, Sondra hated the Reapers. It wasn't anything they did. If anything, they were overly polite, always helping her up the stairs with the carriage, or with grocery packages, always servile and meek in her presence. She simply couldn't believe that after two years as a gutter junkie, a year in prison, all of that, Georgie would start playing kids' games in the street with a bunch of sixteen-year-olds.

In a way, she thought, it was better when it was just the two of them, living off the street. Sure, she had had to make all the decisions, and Georgie had sometimes disgusted her with his weakness and crazy impulses. But at least it was the two of them together, hiding, running, scrapping, stealing, sleeping together. He did what she thought was best, and he did it for both of them.

Now she was stuck caring for the baby, making the pitiful welfare checks last through the month, paying the rent and food bills, paying for his beer and rum, and cleaning up after his friends every time they came up to sit around and trade their boy-child macho stories. The most he would do was go to the store every once in a while to pick up the groceries. He was a big man on the street, though she couldn't understand why, so she was supposed to act the part of his serving woman. She was supposed to be happy with a few hours in the sun, walking the baby and chatting with the fat old women who would surround her on the street and hound her with advice or bore her with gossip.

She fought with him about it constantly. She threatened to move in with her mother and grandmother, who lived in the Southeast Bronx. He never hit her, never really fought back; he would always end the fight by promising to go out and look for a job. Then, for the next few days, he would tell her where he had looked for one, and how this one was cheap and nasty, or this place wanted him to train for no money for a few weeks, and so he couldn't find anything. She would nod and say nothing. Until the next fight.

Georgie spent all his spare time on the street with the Reapers. It reminded him of the good times he had had years ago with the Hawks, only this time it was better. The Reapers didn't have to hide on rooftops or in broken-down apartments in abandoned buildings. They were the number-one clique in the neighborhood, and those who didn't belong made sure they had friends who were Reapers, or they moved out in a hurry. They had a basement that they used as headquarters. They owned their own jackets and even a couple of guns. The street-gang thing was still new to him, but Georgie figured it wasn't much different from the way things had always been. The oldest and toughest dudes always ran the street any way they saw fit. Keep to your own turf was the law of the street. The only differences now were the jackets, which were superfine, and, maybe, the fact that there were so many damn kids on the streets now that the competition had gotten tougher. He felt a lot better wearing his Reaper colors then he ever had sitting on the junkie benches in Crotona Park.

The gang had existed for about a year, forming after several neighborhood kids had been run out of a schoolyard a block south of Tremont by another gang called the Royal Javelins. At first, they were called the Latin Devils and were led by a loud-mouthed and brash seventeen-year-old named Manny. When Eddie got out of prison and moved into the neighborhood, he became involved with the gang through his cousin, who was a member.

Eddie arranged to have the gang join the central division of the Reapers, one of the original South Bronx gangs, and one with a Bronx-wide reputation. In return for their monthly dues, the gang members were issued Reaper colors, a couple of pistols, and a pledge of armed support from all other Reaper divisions should a serious war break out with another gang. Eddie became president of the Fourth Division Reapers, as they were called, and Manny became vice president.

The gang was a fixture on Morton Place. They would patrol the streets at night, wordlessly warning strangers off the block, partly to scare junkies and other thieves away, and partly because it just felt good and tough. Their relations with others in the neighborhood were mixed. Some complained about the no-account punks always hanging on the corner and the stoops, doing nothing but looking for trouble; others, remembering what it was like when they themselves were growing up, were friendlier. Eddie saw to it that things stayed cool with the neighbors; Reapers were forever opening doors and carrying packages for the women in the two apartment buildings on the corner of Morton and Harrison, even though some of them were downright nasty. They watched over the neighborhood children who played in the street during the summer while daylight lasted. They rarely went looking for trouble, even with other gangs; that was the way Eddie had operated his clique in prison, and that was the way he was running the Reapers in the street. Nice and laid back; that was the way he liked it.

As a prison friend of Eddie's, Georgie immediately had special status with the gang membership, and Eddie made that official by giving Georgie the title of war counselor. It was largely ceremonial, since an occasional street fight in a playground was the only kind of war the Fourth Division had to deal with. But they were aware that they were surrounded by neighborhood gangs, all potentially hostile. Individual gang members did not often wear their Reaper colors to Saturday-night parties or on trips outside the neighborhood.

Georgie's friendship with Eddie fueled an already smoldering bitterness in Manny, the gang's vice president. He began challenging Eddie on virtually every decision, and he was always ready with a wisecrack whenever Georgie said anything. Georgie was tempted to call him out more than a couple of times, but Eddie always held him back. Once Eddie told Georgie that he would have to call out Manny himself, sooner or later, but the time had to be right, because he didn't trust Manny not to use a knife or a gun in a street fight.

The gang members began taking sides, and Georgie was afraid that if Eddie didn't act soon, the gang would be at war with itself. They would gather on Morton Place, some twenty-odd Reapers, and some would sit on the stoop next to Eddie, in front of his building, while others would cluster around Manny, across the street on the stairs of the building he lived in. There were more fights and arguments in the basement meetings. Georgie found that some of the Reapers wouldn't talk to him, though most of those were afraid to do the same to Eddie.

Early one morning, Georgie was sitting outside the gang basement with a couple of Reapers, picking his teeth with a metal toothpick, when a car came up Morton Place, slowing down for a moment directly in front of them. One of the back doors was shoved open, and a large bundle came rolling out of the back seat. The door slammed, and the car sped off, turning north on University Avenue.

Georgie and the others ran up and found Joselito, one of the youngest Reapers, sprawled on the pavement. His colors had been slashed in several places and tied around his mouth and throat. He had several cigarette burns on his face and arms, and his collarbone and one of his wrists were broken. A couple of bruised ribs were making it difficult for him to breathe. "Black Spades" was all he could squeeze out when they asked him what had happened.

•

The war with the Black Spades lasted four months, and at one time during that period, it felt to Georgie like the whole stinking Bronx was at war. It was his first contact with a street war. Though he had been in several fights when he was younger, had seen more than his share of bodies in forgotten alleys, and had witnessed a couple of killings, fighting with a gun or a knife was new to him. He bought a short-blade knife and practiced in front of a mirror with it when Sondra wasn't around. It felt right in his hands, but he remembered the bloody, leaking, balloon-like face of the cook at Woodburn, and he wondered what it would be like to sink the blade into flesh and bone and see the thick red liquid gush out.

The whole thing started downtown, when the Black Spades and the Secret and Imperial Bachelors went to war over drug territory. Other gangs became involved because of previous alliances or because, as the war got more violent, their own territory was violated. The Spades had more divisions then any other gang in the Bronx, and the Bachelors had several also, and the time came when no gang member was safe wearing his colors on any block in the Bronx.

The Reapers stopped wearing their colors at night, even on their own street. Georgie wouldn't let Sondra on the street after dark, though she thought the whole thing was stupid. Once, a young Reaper who had just joined the gang practically crawled into the gang basement one morning. Georgie was there; he had spent the night in the basement after another fight with Sondra. The kid fell down the steps and rolled against the wall. "Que pasa?" Georgie asked him, but the kid turned his face to the wall. He started mumbling, and Georgie had to lean over him to hear. Georgie asked him five or six times to roll over so he could hear him better. Then he realized that the kid was crying and didn't want Georgie to see. Later, he discovered that the kid had been tied to a tree and beaten with baseball bats; half of his ribs were cracked, and the lower half of his torso was a mass of blue-black bruises.

Eddie wanted no more of this, and he ordered that colors not be worn unless the gang was together, and that members were to be armed with knives or shark's wheels (brass knuckles with teeth like a machine gear) at all times. Manny saw this as an opportunity to make his move, and he disregarded the order, wearing his colors all the time, until they stank with his sweat. One August night, he was heading home from a cousin's house, walking on Harrison Avenue, when he was suddenly knocked down from behind. He turned and saw a Black Spade, wearing colors, holding a German shepherd on a thick leather leash. The dog was practically at his throat when a jerk on the leash pulled him away. Then the dog backed him into an alleyway and against a garage door. The Spade started swinging a heavy chain—not a bicycle chain, but a thick, heavy fence chain. After two or three swings, Manny sank to his knees; then he fell on all fours. He began to vomit blood. The Spade backed off for a second, clenching the dog's leash in one hand and the chain in the other. The dog was pulling wildly, the smell of the blood driving it mad. Suddenly a Reaper named Panama appeared in the alleyway, holding a sawed-off shotgun. He screamed at the Spade to stop swinging the chain. The Spade turned and started slowly twirling the chain around his head as he walked toward Panama. He shouted at the dog to turn and attack the new intruder. Panama fired one barrel of the gun. The dog whimpered and fell dead. The chain swung slowly to a halt, as the Spade stood dumfounded, staring at the dead animal. Panama stood frozen in fear; his hand was still pointing the gun toward the body of the dog.

Suddenly, Manny sprang up and ran toward them. Screaming, "Shoot him, shoot him, you stupid pussy!" Manny grabbed the gun, turned and fired the second barrel into the Spade's chest. The shock spun the Spade around and against the alley wall; then he fell dead into a pool of blood: Manny's, the dog's, his own.

Manny threw the gun down and ran out of the alley, brushing Panama aside. Panama stayed for a few more seconds, then turned and ran, too. Lights

were on and people were running on the street.
Many people saw Manny and then Panama come
running out of the alley; some of them knew exactly
who they were. But by the time the police sirens
were whining to a halt on Harrison Avenue, both of
them had disappeared into the Bronx night, to ride
buses and trains until each of them caught his breath
and could decide what to do.

The police rounded up every Reaper they could
find. None of the members knew anything about
what had happened; they just knew from the gossip
on the street that Panama and Manny had come running out of the alleyway where the remains of the
Spade and his dog were found. Georgie was terrified,
because he thought for sure that the cops would
question him at length and then check on his record
—and that would mean a trip back to Woodburn for
parole violation. He stayed inside his house for three
days, waiting for the knock on the door.

But the police had strong identifications of
Manny and Panama from several eyewitnesses, and
most of the Reapers questioned about the murder
had nervously fingered the two of them by slipping
the fact of their disappearance into casual conversation. Nobody came to talk to Georgie, because they
didn't need Georgie to tell them what everybody
else had already told them.

Panama was picked up on a panhandling charge
on Fordham Road, then transferred to the Bronx
Street Gang Task Force headquarters. Manny was
picked up in Orchard Beach Park after he pulled out
a knife and then ran from a cop who was going to

throw him off the beach for vagrancy. He was also brought to the Task Force Unit. The two were questioned for several hours, together and separately. The police knew that the weapon belonged to Panama, and they were more interested in him than in Manny: Panama had a record of two arrests, one of them on a weapons charge, while Manny was clean. They worked on Manny to get him to turn on Panama. They told him he might get off completely.

Two days later, Manny was back on the street. He was friendly and very talkative. He was out, home free. Panama would probably be out, too, in a few days. "Self-defense, man," Manny said. "That motherfucking dog was gonna rip his fucking throat out. What else could he do? I would've stabbed him if Panama didn't shoot him."

Georgie was sure that Manny was full of crap. But Eddie didn't say anything, so Georgie didn't either. For the next couple of days, everyone would fall silent when Manny came around. He would chatter on about everything under the sun, and nobody else would say anything, except an occasional "Yeah, Manny," or a nod of the head.

Sometime after midnight, a couple of weeks after the killing, Eddie rang Georgie's bell. After apologizing in polite Spanish to Sondra, he sat Georgie down in the kitchen and told him what he had found out. Panama was up on a murder rap. Manny had fingered him, even though people who thought they had seen the two of them in the alley before they came running out were pretty sure that Manny had thrown away a gun before he ran out. Panama, they said, seemed just to stand there for a moment, then turned and ran out.

Eddie coldly explained what he thought they might do. They could kill Manny and just try to get away with it. Or they could kill Manny and try to pin it on the Black Spades. Or they could just turn him over to the Black Spades and let them decide what to do with him.

"No," Georgie said quickly, thinking that he wasn't quite ready for a murder rap. "That would mean more trouble." He thought for a moment. "We got to scare him, scare him bad. We'll scare that pussy until he won't show his face on the street again."

Late one Saturday night, while Manny was asleep, drunk, on the couch in his brother's apartment, where he lived, five wide-mouthed Rheingold chug-amug bottles stuffed with rags soaked in gasoline were lit and thrown into the window of the apartment. They exploded with a flash, and everything in the room began to burn. Drunk as he was, Manny was awakened by the sound of the breaking window and managed to drag himself into the street, burned but alive. Mysteriously, the fire alarm switch on the corner had been pulled in time to keep the fire from spreading to other buildings. The apartment was gutted, and everything in it was destroyed, but nobody else got hurt. Manny's brother moved to Queens, and Manny went with him.

The war with the Spades had one other casualty. One of Manny's neighbors had seen three boys running down the street just before the flames burst through the windows of the apartment next to his.

He could only see one of them, he said. He looked a little older than the other two. Light-skinned guy, with black hair, Spanish face. Could be any one of a dozen guys around the block.

But the cops had an idea of who it might be. They booked Eddie on suspicion of arson; because of his record, high bail was set, and he was carted off to Riker's Island. When the Reapers gathered at the basement to discuss what to do, with both Eddie and Manny gone, it was Georgie they turned to for the final word.

Georgie was no street fighter. In prison he had punched out a couple of dudes who tried to walk on him because they found out he was a junkie, but he was not a street fighter. His whole life style as a junkie had been geared toward avoiding violence, especially after he had hooked up with Sondra. But his years of climbing fences, balancing on thin parapets, running through dark and narrow alleys, leaping from rooftop to rooftop, had developed him physically into a street-toughened cat of a man-child. His dope years had thinned every ounce of fat out of him; now his time away from dope gave his body rock-hard definition. He was older and knew his way around a lot better than the other gang members. Some of them had first-hand knowledge of Georgie's skills: trapped with three others by a half dozen Spades on their way back from a meeting with the Park Avenue Reapers, Georgie had led them up to the roof of a building. The Spades were right behind them when they reached the roof door. Holding the door open with one hand, Georgie stayed behind and, with one arm, shoved the first Spade down the steep staircase and into the others. Then he led the other Reapers from rooftop to rooftop, up and down stairwells, until they came out a long block northeast from where they started, with no pursuit in sight. "He don't scare easy," one of them had told Manny later. "He ran, didn't he?" Manny had snapped. "You would, too, man," was the answer.

No one voted no when Georgie was elected the new president of the Fourth Division Reapers.

In early April, sometimes late in March, when the nights are no longer frozen and bone chilling, and the damp spring breeze begins to drift in from the south, the dark and barren concrete landscape of the Bronx grows people. At first little groups of twos and threes, walking down wide avenues in long tweed coats, looking from a distance like shriveled old men, protected by the thick membrane of cloth, until the telltale swivel action from the hips, the cool sashaying, gives them away. Like hibernating animals, the young men emerge from their tenement caves and walk to the liquor stores for gin and rum and Yago Sangria, and Boone's Farm Wild Mountain Wine. The coats are absurd; there is nothing hip or fashionable about them. They are simply functional and, as such, timeless.

Nobody wears these coats closed anymore on early spring nights in the Bronx. The danger is past;

they are worn just because it doesn't pay to trust the weatherman, or for that matter, even the calendar. If it were to snow in July, everyone here knows it would snow first and worst in the Bronx. They meet on street corners, and the feeling is of a long separation. "Hey, baby, how you doin'? Goddamn, man, where you been keeping yourself?" And in many cases the separation is real. Cold winter nights are not conducive to hanging out, indoors or outdoors. There are too many people in each apartment to soak up the precious warmth, seeping through the pipes of the radiators. Friendships here must stand the test of infrequent contact more than of time. Friends can see each other ten hours a day for six months, and then not get together at all for four months.

A few minutes chatting on the street corner, and someone says, "Let's get something for the head." A short migration to the liquor store follows. Liquor stores in the South Bronx are models of successful free enterprise in a hostile urban environment. There is no contact whatsoever between consumer and product. He passes through the doors and finds himself in a glass-and-steel-enclosed waiting room, as in a bank or a small betting parlor. There is a window at the far end, and there behind it, sitting on a stool, is the owner or his helper. In the center of the window is a square opening that reveals a circular platform which can pivot 360 degrees. It is divided into semicircles by a thick sheet of plastic. An order is placed by shouting through the opening. Then the money is placed on one half of the platform, and the liquor and the change come back on the other half.

No one seems to mind this anymore, this faceless way of doing business, for it has become a fact of life. Everyone accepts that fact of life. After all, even junkies are hassled by other junkies. And everyone has a story about someone being shot up or cut up for a few dollars and change. Every man can handle a little street confrontation, but the crazies can catch anyone by surprise.

There are lines of overcoats, two and three deep, talking quietly in hushed tones, sometimes laughing out loud or cackling Bill Russell style, but somewhat muted, as if at a wake or a church bazaar. There are few hostile faces on this line. No one seems to mind the wait; even at eleven o'clock at night there are three or four little groups huddled in a ragged line, refilling for the fourth and fifth time. Sometimes two little groups merge into one larger group. "Where you been keeping yourself, bro?" And the voices become louder and more open. There is a brief silence as the money and liquor exchange, and they all drift back out into the night, unified by the long, wrinkled brown bag that one of them is carrying.

A swing up the street and back to a building entrance way, then into a dark corner where someone, maybe a couple of young chicks, or even someone's older sister, is waiting, seated on a rickety bridge chair or a wooden milk carton, waiting with the FM radio turned up full volume, pounding a cacophony of eclecticism, a Willy Bobo–Temptations–Stones–Isaac Hayes–Carly Simon–Herbie Hancock–nonstop blend of pounding sound. The hand at the station knob is always restless, never happy; two and a half minutes of raw sound pour through the cold and tinny speakers—little hoarse speakers that never once correct the sound, but instead just let the noise pour through, a little coarser for the journey. Then a lightning-quick journey through a hundred voices and sounds, with a flash stop here and there, an impatient hesitation, waiting for the glib voice to stop talking and get the sound moving again. And then finally another brief rest. Ninety seconds of the tail-end of something-or-other, and then off again, up and down the band, in search of more and better sound.

But no matter—the drums, the bass, the wine are always there; the blood simmers in the sound and the night and the liquor and the voices. Someone occasionally screeches along, trying to match the volume. Others are huddled in the corner, rapping to this chick or that, or grabbing a look at a pornographic book, "From Europe, man," that somebody snatched. Picture after picture of genitals, sometimes five and six to a picture, and, incredibly, no faces, no breasts even, as if the photographer had used a special lens to zero in on a twelve-inch cross-section of the human body. The colors are flat and sickly, like the tenement walls in the dark building behind. Someone tells a story about how this and that old man never even puts it to his wife. He just lies in the bed all day and beats his meat, to the slow tune of these sad and lifeless, nearly unidentifiable organs. And everyone laughs. But everyone looks anyhow.

As the evening wears on, the shrill siren calls of squad cars and ambulances and fire trucks pierce through the mass of wailing sound with some regularity. Someone turns the volume down, and there is sudden quiet. Eyes are open now. Is it coming closer? When it does, everyone ventures out a little from the corner to the courtyard, peering into the night. If the sound keeps coming, everyone walks slowly out toward the street and peers toward the sound, a little anxious and a little excited. It seems like more than half of those out after dark have bench warrants out for their arrest, mostly for nonappearance in a misdemeanor trial, or for parole or probation violations. They know, of course, that no fleet of squad cars is going to come roaring up the street to get them. Most likely they'll get it when they get hassled by a couple of bored station-house cruisers who have to break balls by phoning the precinct and checking the sheet rundown on them. But they're scared anyhow. And they hate being scared, because all that good feeling, all that roaring, burning, high feeling, just dissipates as, steeled and tense, everyone waits for the siren to show.

An ambulance or a fire truck relaxes everyone. If it stops nearby, the carnival is turned on and everyone joins in, chattering and laughing, moving en masse to where the vehicle is stopped, ignoring pleas to stand aside, idly watching, asking, "Who got it this time?" Is he old or young? Was it an OD, or a heart attack, or just a stabbing, or someone burned with lye, or is it just the bad DTs, or a broken hip falling down the stairs because the creaky old elevator went dead again?

And oh, how the firemen and ambulance attendants hate these people! These animals, who throw bricks and bottles at them, who laugh at their bright red faces, who seem to revel in death and destruction. What kind of people are they, anyway? They cheer and celebrate when a building burns, for Chrissakes. It's like some kind of pagan rite. Don't they care about their own homes; don't they care about the people inside? Returning to the firehouse or to the hospital, they sit and pick at cold beans, a bit of coffee, and mutter about niggers and jungles and animals, really, animals.

But if it is the cops, the crowd becomes quiet and irritable. They turn chilly cold and silent, waiting, watching, defensive, sullen. Usually nothing really happens. Maybe some hysterical old lady phoned the precinct house and screamed into the phone that something really nasty was going on next door, someone was getting killed, Officer, I'm a citizen too. You'd better get here. Just because we're black folks here don't mean we ain't got a right to live decent. And if she hasn't called too often before, a squad car or two goes screaming into the night and wheels screeching up to the apartment house. The woman is on the street waiting, wild-eyed; a crowd has already gathered around her, encircled her, keeping a respectful distance. After all, she may be crazy. She is wearing a bathrobe over a long nightgown, and fur slippers; sweat gleams on her forehead. "What took you so long, Officer?" she asks. "Come this way." And the cop, very young, very working-class Irish, feeling totally the fool, resentment building steadily inside him, follows her into the building, his hand already itching for his gun. He is as much frightened by this witch of a woman as by the crowd outside, remembering now the station-house stories about the guy who went on one of these routine calls, same broad who had called for the fiftieth time, and he never drew his gun, just knocked on the door, and, finding it open, stepped in and got his insides blown out by a sawed-off shotgun.

He knocks on the door, nervous, angry. "Anyone in here?" he says. "Police." And he hears creaks and groans, and reads frightful meanings into them. His palm is wet, and it's all he can do to keep from whipping that gun out and blowing the lock off. "Open up, goddamn it, or I'm coming in!" he finally shouts, and some sleepy-looking old guy in a T shirt opens the door.

An angry face, like an old dog. A barrelful of fat for a stomach, coffee stains all over the faded white cotton. "What you motherfuckers want me for?" he says. "Can't you leave us alone? Is that ugly bitch next door brought this on? I'll skin her!" "Don't you be calling me that, you black devil, drinking and carrying on up here all the time! Ain't you got no shame, living like an animal the way you do?"

The cop wants to hit them both, he is so sick of them. There are only two kinds of spics and niggers, he thinks—the religious fanatics and the ones who drink and screw and shoot up and waste themselves and each other. But instead, in a flat, nasal New Yorkese, he takes charge, feigning boredom mixed with a little anger. He tells them both to shut up. "Let me just look around, friend," he says, mocking friendship

slightly, but smiling broadly. "After all, I got a report
to fill out." But the man is sweating. His face is brooding. And again the shotgun-blast dream fills up the
cop's mind, and his hand twitches for his gun. Instead, he flips his club around, and, seeing that, the
fear flashes in the black man's eyes. A minute's silence, and then the black man sighs. "Go ahead, look,
but just tell that bitch to mind her own business from
now on. It's getting to be so's a man can't drink in his
own house." He mutters some more to himself and
turns away.

The cop drifts through ragged rooms, with bare
and stained mattresses, and walls that look like a
relief map of the ocean floor. A tiny stove, a filthy
bathroom, a stink in the air that breathes of no fresh
air since last October. In one bedroom he sees a
woman sprawled on a bed, half naked; her dress
shows her black thighs all the way to her crotch. She
lies with no apparent thought to modesty or to comfort. And again the cop tightens in alert fear. She's
dead, he thinks, and that crazy black son of a bitch
is behind me with a butcher knife, ready to cut a grin
in the back of my neck, ready to drink my good white
Irish blood. Turn slow now, be cool, he thinks, and he
turns fast, and scared, gun drawn, and sees nothing.
Lucky for him. Had the man been behind him, he
might have shot and killed him, over his drunken
wife, for nothing.

On the way out, the cop meets his partner, gun
in hand, coming down the hall. "Yes, everything is all
right," he says. "There was nothing there but a couple of drunken niggers and that old biddy." The

backup unit has arrived and is controlling the crowd, his partner assures him. The cop's neck is red as he walks out of the building, hearing the taunts of faceless voices thrown at him. The crowd is angry because it has been disappointed. They have come out empty-handed, no hero to save, no prisoner to protect. And, wordless, the cops walk back to their cars, the radios squawk in the eerie silence, the cars dribble away from the curb and the crowd drifts apart in the same twos and threes again, back to the shadowed corners.

And so the nights pass with a kind of festive sameness. As the weather gets warmer, the streets get thicker with people. The little kids stay out into the late hours, filling the night with the sound of scratching roller skates, high-pitched yells, and moaning whines, and occasionally somebody's mother shouts a name from a window, one, two, three times, and then a long "Whaaat" comes wailing up to answer her, followed by a conversation that no one else can understand. Mothers sit on the steps of buildings feeding their babies on warm milk and warm little breezes that come up when the sun goes down behind Manhattan.

On weekends the streets are emptier, cleaned out by the lure of Saturday night—parties and movies and after-hours clubs. The booze is fancier, and so is the clothing. It's high-stepping time, costume time. Out come frilly shirts in outrageous shades of orange and pink and maroon. Out come the high-waisted wide-belled pants, and little sexy tops, and the five-inch platform shoes in green and red and brown and black, a rainbow of feet against the dirty, wet pavement. The scene is more frenetic on the weekends, more tense. There is less of a sense of relaxation than an aura of challenge. This is the busiest night in station houses and emergency rooms. This is the night for assault and rape and brutal murder, the night that gave the tinny little handgun the tacky name "Saturday-night special." This is the night when the weekday game of insults flashing back and forth is not played by the same rules. Wisecracks on weekdays bring forth smiles and a little playful wrestling. The same lines on a Saturday night have an extra cutting edge to them that starts the adrenaline flowing. Seems like everyone has spent the week just practicing for Saturday night; even the junkies and the winos try to get it together for this night. There is an orgasmic desperation in it.

Then the summer comes, and the warm weather is here to stay, and Saturday night is every night.

XIV

Georgie is standing on the sidewalk on Morton Place, in the middle of the block, holding a wooden broom handle in his hand. He is drowning in sweat. It is a hot, muggy day with a yellowing sky; the air stinks, but Georgie is playing stickball. Just he and Luis.

On the gray wall behind him is a yellow box with an X in it. This is Luis's target. Luis hides the pink ball behind him, forty feet away in the middle of the street. He winds. He throws, sidearm. The ball is a pink blur. Georgie swings and misses. Swinging and missing is all he has been doing for the last hour, except when he hasn't swung at all. They've been playing for one hour, and when the ball and the bat have connected, it's been an accident. There have been three accidents during that hour. All have been foul tips. And Georgie and Luis keep on playing. Kapop. Ball four. Whoosh. Strike three. And they change places and start all over again.

About eight or nine Reapers are sitting across the street, thirty feet or so behind Luis. They stare straight ahead, so that it is impossible to tell whether they are mesmerized by the heat and their own boredom, or whether they are so intent on watching the stickball game that they have lost all track of time and space. All of them are soaking in their own sweat, and none of them asks to get into the game.

Georgie swings, and the bat goes sploosh against the ball—a miracle—and the ball sails into the air, wobbling in an oblong shape, an eggball. Luis races for it and misses. It hits the ground, takes a crazy bounce, and rolls all the way down the street. Someone down the street picks it up and throws it back, but the rubber ball is cracked at the seam. The ball game is over.

Georgie walks over to the sidewalk and sits down in front of the gang basement. "You must be high on your own sweat, man," somebody says to him, and he smiles. He goes inside, comes back with a towel and a beer, and sits down against the wall. Another of the Reapers has arrived with a basketball, and a three-on-three game is about to start. The basket is wired to a square piece of wood that has been nailed to a telephone pole. It doesn't sit just right, there is no net, and the telephone pole sits just six inches away from the curb on the sidewalk, so that anyone who comes crashing in for a layup or a rebound can catch his foot on the sidewalk and wrench a knee, or come crashing down on the concrete. But it's better than the milk crate they used for a basket last year.

The game begins, and the action's fast. Ten baskets, and the sides change. Ten baskets take a long time, especially since every once in a while the ball goes through the hoop, hits the point of the concrete sidewalk, and goes caroming down the street. Georgie watches, but he doesn't play. He still hates basketball. The younger Reapers tease him about it. Basketball is an obsession on the street. In between games, they bait Georgie until he smiles and gets up and walks out into the street. The ball is passed to him. He fumbles it. He bounces it twice, awkwardly. Then he throws a weird two-handed jump shot, shotputting it from his right shoulder. The ball smashes against the wood backboard and, missing the rim, sails over everybody's head and down the street. Everybody laughs, and Georgie, still smiling, sits down.

There are no cars on Morton Place. No parked cars, no traffic. Down by Harrison Avenue is a ragged row of police barricades and garbage cans, blocking off the street. Georgie has decreed the street a play street. Kids of all sizes are playing scully and catch, roller skating and tag in the middle of the street. Some are the brothers and sisters of gang members. Some are the children of gang members. All of them play carelessly under the gang's relaxed but vigilant eye.

Once in a while, a frustrated gypsy cab driver, who has turned up Harrison to beat the traffic on Tremont and who wants to cut up Morton to get to University, will stop his cab, slam the door, stalk over to the barricade, and start to move it out of the way. He will then become aware that there is a sudden silence on the street. The children have stopped playing and are staring at him. If he glances up the street, he will see a dozen sullen faces glaring at him from stoops and sidewalks.

Then Georgie will go into his act. He walks slowly up the street, his stringy biceps taut against his brown skin, and, grinning with his teeth, says, "What the hell you doin', man?" The guy looks at his hands. "This street is closed, man. Can't you see the little children playing here, man? Ain't you got eyes, man?" The cabby looks down the street. He rubs his neck. Jesus, is this grinning bastard going to cut me up? he thinks. "We don't want any trouble, man," Georgie says, as if reading his mind. "Why don't you just get back into the cab and drive up to Burnside? Be cool, man." He puts his arm around the guy and guides him back to his cab, still smiling. The cabby is smiling too, though a bit nervously. And all of them laugh as the cab shoots up the street, and Georgie returns to the stoop.

Exhausted, the basketball players walk back to the sidewalk and sit down. Georgie scrounges up a couple of dollars and sends someone around the corner for a couple of quart bottles of Colt 45. The players sit and soak, until the slight breeze slowly sucks up the moisture. Somebody makes a comment about somebody else's mother. He gets a fake punch to the face and a knee in the stomach for an answer. They spar around the sidewalk, fists flying. One of them lands a punch, and they start to wrestle. Locked in each other's arms, they squeeze, until one breaks free and runs a few steps away. Then they sit down again.

"You see that last shot? Vrroooom! Twenty-foot

line drive, clean in. Like my man, Jerry West. Jump shot. Vrooom. Swish. Clean in."

"Jerry West, man? You play more like Binky East. Next time, look when you shoot the ball, and you'll miss like you always do."

"C'mon, sucker, I'll take you on right now. One on one. I'll shit all over you."

"You got to clean it off yourself first."

Silence.

"Hey, you remember when that sucker West put in an eighty-five-foot jump shot?"

"Eighty-five feet! Get the fuck outta here. You shoot more jive than any man alive."

"Yeah, well, I seen it on TV. Against the Knicks. The Knicks are down, see, by ten or twelve, but they catch up, and DeBusschere puts in a tap with, like, three seconds to go, and the Knicks are winning by two. And Chamberlain throws the ball into West, and he walks away, because he knows the game is over, see. But West, he takes two steps and he lets it fly, and the ball hits the backboard, and bam! it goes right in. And my man DeBusschere is at the other end, just in case, see, and when he see it go in, like, he faints, you dig, he, like, just falls right over. Eighty-five feet. Man, that sucker can shoot."

"Eighty-five feet. Where you make this shit up from, Binky? You got a machine at home?"

"I seen it, man. I ain't lyin'. Ask Johnson. He seen it too. Tell him, Johnson."

Johnson shrugs, because he's heard the story so many times, he's not sure anymore whether he's seen it or not. Then someone starts on another story.

It was the summer of Georgie's first year as president of the Reapers, and it was a quiet summer, quiet enough to drive them all crazy. Since the shooting during the war with the Black Spades, the Fourth Division had enjoyed a reputation as the baddest gang in the West Bronx. None of the local gangs was too anxious to challenge them. They were a little sheepish about that, or at least the older members were. The younger ones were content with embellishing the stories of the war, and their parts in them, to impress the members who had only just joined.

The turnover in any street gang is enormous from summer to summer, and the Reapers were no exception. It's not only the shootings, the stabbings, and the busts. Families move away, frightened by the bloodstains on the concrete and the screams in the night, and they take their kids with them, even the ones who wear colors and carry knives. Boys grow into men overnight, and the fragile games of the street become boring, and they look for different ways to pass the time. Friendships are tentative and are governed by the seasons.

At least half the Reapers' membership was new that summer, and most of them knew Georgie only as a legendary hero from the Great War. The gang's initiation rite tended to embellish his reputation. A new member had to fight Georgie one-to-one, until one of them quit. And it was never Georgie who quit. His reputation grew until it was considered an act of great courage simply to agree to the initiation. New gang members won their own reputations on the basis of how they fared in their fight with Georgie.

Georgie thrived on all that attention, and he played the part of the street prince. He bought himself a cane with a carved mahogany handle. The handle unscrewed, and then served as the hilt for a triangular sword, sharpened on all three corners. As a weapon it was impractical, but it was great for show. He wore flowery shirts and tight black pants at night; in the daytime, muscle-tight T shirts showed off his wiry frame to best advantage. But his real joy was his colors. He wore a cutoff dungaree jacket, like the others, with the same insignia emblazoned on the back: The Grim Reaper with the words REAPERS BRONX surrounding it. But around the neck, and climbing down the buttonholes to his waist, was a luxurious fur collar, soft and beautiful. He wore his colors only on very special occasions, like parleys with other gangs, or with the leaders of the Central Division Reapers. Or when he was trying to impress some fox on the street.

He was on the street more than he was home, as much because he didn't want to be home as because he loved being outside. Sondra barely spoke to him anymore. He had given up all pretense of looking for a job, and they lived on the welfare money she collected every month. Twice, Sondra had been convinced he was going to change and give up this second childhood of his. The first time came when he was out driving a car he had borrowed from a neighbor. He didn't have a license, and he didn't know where to get one, but he had learned how to drive while he was in prison, and would occasionally borrow a car whenever he had to run an errand over to

Sondra's mother's house, on the other side of the Bronx.

He was in an accident, and the driver of the other car jumped out of his car and called him a gorilla and a dirty spic. Enraged, Georgie beat the larger man unmercifully. It took a couple of policemen to subdue him, and he was booked on a number of charges, including assault with a deadly weapon (his knife, which they found in his pocket). They discovered he had a record, and his parole officer was called in.

Georgie had to see his p.o. once a month. They usually spent most of that time arguing over Georgie's getting a job. The p.o. would threaten to send Georgie back to prison if he didn't stop hanging around with the Reapers and if he didn't make a serious effort to find work. Georgie would scream that he was healthy, he was happy, he was off dope, what more could he want? The p.o. usually left it hanging, more as a threat than anything else, because he was pleased that Georgie showed no signs of the needle, and that, for the time being, he hadn't gotten into any more trouble.

When the parole officer read the report on the fight and the accident and heard Georgie's version, he felt inclined to try to get him off. Sounds like the guy in the other car got what was coming to him, he thought. But he wasn't going to lift a finger for Georgie without exacting something in return. He made Georgie promise to stay away from the Reapers. He increased the number of times that Georgie had to report to twice a month. He told him that he had to have a job within six weeks, or it was back to Wood-burn, or worse. In return, he got Georgie out on probation, even though the other driver insisted on pressing the assault charge.

When Georgie got home, Sondra said nothing to him. She was afraid that anything she said would just make him angry. For a couple of days, he sat around the house, watched TV, and played with the kid. One morning, he shaved and dressed and went down to the state employment office to look for work. He didn't get back until late that afternoon, and he was hot and sullen and irritable. The next morning, he got up early, grabbed his cane, and went down to the gang basement before she got out of bed. After that, she saw him even less than before. She didn't find out until much later that he had decided not to report to his p.o. anymore.

Then Sondra found out she was pregnant again. She didn't tell him until she was almost halfway through her term. She wanted to see if he would notice on his own. Finally she had to tell him, because she no longer had the strength to deal with all the chores he left to her. Over the next few months, he paid a lot more attention to her, though not nearly so much as she would have liked. Even so, she felt hope for the first time that they might finally make it. He seemed genuinely happy that he was going to be a father again, and she believed him. For all his faults in her eyes, she never doubted that he loved Cathy, their first child. Even in his worst moods, he was always gentle with her.

Actually, it was easy for Georgie to revel in another child. On the street, getting a woman pregnant was a sign of a true man. Births were cause for celebration in the neighborhood. People married young on Morton Place, and Georgie and the other Reapers were always making courtesy calls on a young Reaper's wife and new baby. They would tramp up the stairs in twos and threes to the girl's mother's house. "She takes after the mother. That's good," Georgie would say, and mother and father would smile shyly. Grandmother would accept their compliments politely, then sigh and tighten her belt, and prepare for another twenty years of raising a family.

Once the baby was born, though, he wasn't so pleased anymore. Georgie hadn't been around when Cathy was born, and by the time he and Sondra got together again, the kid was no longer waking up three times in the middle of the night to screech out her discomfort. Georgie didn't take too well to three A.M. feedings, even if he never was the one who got up and did the feeding. The new baby wasn't two months old when Georgie stopped coming home until one or two in the morning.

Sondra heard rumors about Georgie playing around, but she wrote them off as the usual garbage that passes through a neighborhood grapevine. Georgie did a lot of talking and hustling around the young chicks on the block, but he was hesitant to follow up anything. He was somehow certain that Sondra would find out wherever and whenever he got it on with another woman. He once spent a whole evening rapping to a couple of ripe young sisters. Sharing a quart of wine with them, he found himself drunkenly imagining himself in bed with both of them, screwing the daylights out of them both, the king commanding his slaves to do his bidding. He was within another sip of wine of making his move when Sondra came down the street with a knife in her hand and murder in her eyes. The girls screamed and ran inside, but she kept coming, and she was almost on him before he lurched away, dumbly realizing that she meant to cut him. She managed, in her rage and his drunken fear, only to slash him on the arm, but the scar was there to remind him that Sondra was every bit as tough as he was.

He spent more than a few nights sleeping on the stained mattresses in the gang basement. He could wake up there and see his name in big letters on the wall, bigger than all the rest. The letters screamed his name out at anyone who walked through the door. It was better than waking up in the cold silence of his apartment. And the mattress was more comfortable than the couch at home where he wound up sleeping most of the time.

●

During that quiet summer, the Bronx gang wave was reaching a peak. There were more than a hundred gangs spread throughout the Bronx, and the Fourth Division Reapers were surrounded by other gangs on every side. East across Jerome Avenue was a division of the Peacemakers. South, below Tremont, were the Royal Javelins. West, across University, was a gang called the Henchmen, with whom the Reapers had a special score: the Henchmen used colors that looked very much like the Reapers' colors. And North, between University and Grand Street, on 183rd Street, a division of the Savage Skulls had just moved in.

Among the Bronx gangs, the Savage Skulls had probably the worst reputation. This was not only because they were heavily armed, and wild and tough, and unusually willing to take on any neighboring gang. It was also because they were not above gang rape and woman-beating and torture and outright murder, antics that even some of the worst of the early South Bronx gangs found repulsive.

A young division of the Skulls hung out on Grand Avenue and 183rd Street, about a half mile from Morton Place. They were really Skulls in name only, and, like the Reapers, they kept pretty much to themselves. When a couple of older Skulls from the central division moved into a row of apartment buldings a few blocks north of Grand, on University, they took over the division. Dormant until then, the Skulls, supplied with firearms and division support from other neighborhoods, began to prowl the area, looking for gangs to knock over.

Georgie came down to the clubhouse one morning and found that the rim of the basket had been torn away; in its place, sagging against the telephone pole in the heavy summer air, was a set of Savage Skull colors. He waited until some other Reapers arrived, then told one of them to climb the pole and cut the colors down. They threw them into the street, poured gasoline on them, and set them aflame.

That, of course, didn't solve anything, but Georgie wasn't up for another war like the one with the Spades. If the summer days ran on in endless repetition, he didn't mind; he had enough to think about as it was, without worrying about being able to walk the streets at night. He thought that he could pacify his own people by simply burning the colors. And, he thought, if he ignored what had happened, the Skulls might not bother them again.

He was wrong on both counts. Within a few days, the word had spread along Tremont Avenue that Reapers wearing colors would be stomped on sight. The Reapers shrugged it off as just a rumor and went on with their business as if nothing had happened. Georgie pretended to himself that he hadn't heard anything. Then Luis, an old friend of Eddie's who served as Georgie's vice president, was jumped by four Skulls at the Jerome Avenue subway. He was beaten severely, and his colors were torn off his back with his own carpet knife.

There was no way Georgie could avoid facing off the Skulls now. The younger Reapers, who had not yet tasted the fear of seeing death hiding behind every row of garbage cans and in every alleyway, were anxious to dip their still-shiny colors into the gore and glory of a real gang war. The gang gathered at the basement to discuss their next move.

"Let's stomp 'em," a new member of the Reapers, usually quiet to the point of sullenness, said. "We head down Harrison, say, about half of us, and the others circle up around back of University, and we squeeze 'em at Grand. That way, none of them motherfuckers can get out."

"They got a hellifyin' lot of firepower, man," said another. "We ain't got nothing but a couple of pussy specials. They find out we comin', and the lead'll be leavin' Reaper Red all over the gutter."

"Jungle war, then. Ambushes. Rooftop stuff. Shit, man, we got to do somethin'."

Georgie listened, but said nothing. They continued to argue over what to do, but they knew Georgie would have to have the last word. Conversation died, and they looked at him.

"Che," Georgie said finally. "We got to get Che."

Che was a former Fourth Division Reaper who had moved east to the railroad tracks on Park Avenue and had formed his own division of the Reapers. He talked slick, moved fast, and was as hard-nosed as anyone on Morton Place. Georgie and Luis took a walk down Tremont to find Che.

They found him lounging outside his building, talking to his vice president, a big, baby-faced kid named Giganto. He knew what they were there for. One of his Reapers had been beaten by the Skulls a few days ago, and he, too, had been waiting them out. "We didn't dig it too tough, man, but fuckin' with the Skulls ain't everyday business," he said. "We were gonna lay low for a while."

"We better check it out with the central division," Georgie told him. "Until we get the word, tell your studs to be cool. I'll meet you tonight, and we'll tip on over there."

"Che be there. You be there, too."

Like the other big gangs in the South Bronx, the central Reapers suffered under intensive police surveillance. Since the war between the Bachelors and the Black Spades, the big gangs had shied away from open and deliberate conflict. "Do what you want to do," Georgie and Che were told, "and if the shit flies, we'll give you what we can. But don't turn into no pussy division."

Georgie put the word out, through someone who had a cousin in the Skulls, that he wanted a parley. The Skulls answered by sending over three of their younger members. It was a deliberate insult, forcing Georgie to bargain with kids five years his junior who did not speak for the new Skull leadership. The meeting broke down in a series of shouted threats and counterthreats.

The streets emptied out over the next couple of days. Word traveled fast that another war was brewing, and mothers kept their children inside, or called them in long before daylight had faded. The Reapers gathered, as always, in front of the basement each morning, but they were restless, brooding. Only two or three would venture out into the street for a basketball game.

One day, a white kid came walking slowly out of an alleyway in the middle of the block. Beyond the alley were two burned-out, abandoned cars that the kids on the block used for monkey bars. Beyond that, perched on a hill, was an old causeway that cut diagonally away from University Avenue, toward 183rd Street.

The kid leaned against the building and watched the Reapers sitting motionless across the street. For a few minutes, he went unnoticed, just another small figure on the block. Then he turned and hurried toward University, but not before someone noticed the skull and crossbones configuration on the back of his denim jacket.

Before Georgie could say a word, a group of Reapers rushed up the street and surrounded the kid. He stood there, nervously, his hands up, while Georgie pushed through the crowd and faced him.

"What you doin' here, bro'?" Georgie said.

"Just walkin' through, man. It's a free country."

"Watch your mouth, man. Why you wearing Skull colors?"

"These ain't Skull colors, man. It's just a decoration I put on my jacket."

The Reapers were ready to stomp him and leave him for dead on the sidewalk. Out of the corner of his eye, Georgie saw hands in pockets and knew the kid was a few seconds away from getting cut.

"He ain't no Skull," Georgie said, to himself, then, louder, "Let him go. The colors don't look right. He ain't no Skull." And to the kid: "You tip, fast, and don't come back. The next time is the last time."

The hot days dragged on, and the tension got on everybody's nerves. The gang started hanging out in a little vest-pocket park, at the corner of University and Morton, where the old causeway began. They would sit down on the tall grass, first carefully hunting for dog turds, and toke on some weed to cool themselves out a bit. One muggy afternoon, while the threat of a thunderstorm drifted in lazily from the western sky, they were lying out on the grass when one of the kids on the block came running up, breathlessly, to tell Georgie that a strange car was on the block, with three black guys in it. Another black guy had gotten out and gone into one of the corner apartment buildings.

Georgie told Johnson to walk down to the basement and get out the gun they kept under one of the mattresses. "We'll give you five minutes," he said, "and then we're coming down." Nervously, they waited; then, at Georgie's signal, they started down the block, in lines of three, with Georgie in front.

The guys in the cars weren't Savage Skulls, nor were they members of any small-time street gang. They were waiting for their boss to make a numbers pickup and get the hell out of there. He picked a different location every week to collect his money, and this week he had picked an apartment on Morton Place. When they saw the Reapers coming down the street, fanning out purposefully, they started doing what they were paid to do. The driver gunned the engine. The two others pulled out .38's and waited.

Georgie was about thirty feet from the car when one of the men fired out the window at him. Everybody dived for the pavement. The second man began firing out of his window. Johnson suddenly appeared, crouched down on the steps of the basement, and started firing back. Faces appeared at every window, and the screams of mothers shouting at their children shot through the air.

Reapers were crawling along the sidewalk, looking for sticks, rocks, bottles, anything they could use to throw back. A black man came flying out of the building next to the car. There was an almost painful squeal from the tires, and the car leaped toward University. The two men pulled their guns back and stopped shooting as the car gained speed. As the car swept by, Georgie suddenly leaped up and threw a garbage can at it. The can clanged harmlessly against the front fender and rolled noisily away. Then they were gone.

Nobody was hit by anything, bullets or debris. But a lot of the Reapers were not quite as anxious to go to war as they had been before. To Georgie, the whole thing was a case of a lot of nervous dudes and bad overreaction.

A few days later, Johnson and a couple other Reapers caught a Skull named Johnny walking on Harrison Avenue. He was brought back to the gang basement and slit on the cheek with a razor blade. They stripped his colors and told him to go back home and stay out of Reaper territory. That night, Georgie got a call from the central division. The central Skulls had called their division off. They wanted no part of a boroughwide war with the Reapers. As suddenly as it had started, the "war" was over.

Georgie was proud of the fact that he had kept the gang in abeyance until older, cooler heads prevailed. He made a point of going home just to tell Sondra the good news. Sondra said that she didn't really give a damn and asked him when he was going to get a job. Georgie realized that if she had said that to him a year ago, he would have been angry, perhaps even to the point of slapping her. Now he only felt hurt.

It was to be another summer of stickball and

basketball and endless days of waiting out the summer heat. It seemed to Georgie that all his life had been that way; waiting for the next season and whatever hope it might bring.

XV

It is difficult to say whether the street-gang wave has already peaked and begun to fade. This year, some street-gang-related crimes have gone down; others have gone up. The other boroughs claim many street gangs of their own, and the center of big-time activity now seems to be Brooklyn, where, police claim, three or four large gangs control neighborhoodwide protection rackets that have completely terrorized local merchants. There has even been some official speculation that there are links between Brooklyn gangs and the Blackstone Rangers, a Chicago gang of the early sixties that eventually grew so large that it swallowed up much of Chicago's organized crime businesses and changed its name to the Black P. Stone Ranger Nation. Some former Ranger members have turned up in arrests of Brooklyn gang members.

The Lower East Side in Manhattan was the scene of a bloody war between several black and

Puerto Rican gangs, notably the Dynamite Brothers and the Savage Skulls. Not too long ago, two hundred Queens gang members destroyed a hamburger drive-in when the owner tried to bar them from his property. In the end, the owner refused to press charges.

The Bronx gangs are still very active, and, though their membership numbers are not going up, some of the older gangs are undoubtedly better organized and better armed. Gang members are getting older, and their methods have become more sophisticated, and thus more dangerous. A gang called the Turbans, which consists mostly of Vietnam veterans and which is armed with weaponry stolen from the Army by discharged soldiers, specializes in armed robbery. Gangs like the Savage Skulls, the Black Spades, and the Bachelors continue to war over drug territory, having in effect chased the pushers out and taken the drug trade for their own.

Police estimates are that there are about twenty thousand gang members in the city alone. About half of these are in the Bronx; there are few in still lily-white Staten Island. Street gangs are big police business now; even Staten Island has a gang task force, used mostly to watch over old-fashioned motorcycle gangs. There is a street gang intelligence unit, with agents who are assigned to infiltrate gangs. The Bronx Task Force is large enough to be housed in a two-story precinct house on the Cross Bronx Expressway. State legislative hearings were held on the street-gang phenomenon during the summer of 1974. The legislators heard testimony on gangs armed with knives and pipes right on up to those with M–16's, hand grenades and a bazooka.

Where the street gangs get their weapons is no mystery to the police, but it is difficult for them to do anything about it. Anyone with a car can take a week-end jaunt down to one of the southern border states, like North Carolina, Tennessee, or Kentucky, and come back with a trunkful of small handguns; they don't cost much down there. There used to be sporting-goods outlets upstate where gang members would go to buy large revolvers, but most of these have either been closed or are now under tighter regulation. For those without the means or the inclination to travel south, there are dozens of munitions salesmen who can be contacted easily and who will sell guns of all sizes in bulk. A reporter and a photographer interviewed the Tremont Peacemakers just before they purchased a suitcase full of .22's. When the photographer commented that Robert F. Kennedy had been shot with just such a weapon, Junior, the Peacemaker vice-president, didn't miss a beat. "Yeah," he answered, in his deep bass voice, "but he was shot in the head. We only shoot for the ass."

Police officials also think that, in the past, some radical groups made contact with certain gangs and agreed to provide heavy weaponry in return for fomenting violence on the summer streets. An early gang known as the Five Percenters was rumored to be a fanatic wing of the Black Muslims, dedicated to the murder of all whites, but even the police admit that the racial angle is rarely involved in gang fights.

Gang task force units use all manner of police gadgetry to gather intelligence on the gangs. Helicopters are used to sweep rooftops and search for stores of rocks and firebombs, often pitched from the tops of buildings at unsuspecting patrol cars or on an attacking rival gang. They also keep an aerial watch on movements of large numbers of youths on any of the streets below. Undercover agents are assigned to areas where gang activity is reportedly volatile. A street-gang hot line has been established, which is supposed to function as a way of heading off gang fights. In reality, it has functioned mostly as a way of getting anonymous information on individual gang members. Gang leaders are not afraid of phoning the police to turn in a hated rival. It's a lot safer than declaring war. Police officials also find it relatively easy to crack a murder case when it involves an entire street gang; they find they can crack through the gang's veneer of solidarity and find out who pulled the trigger.

Even the police admit that most of the Bronx street gangs are rather tentative neighborhood cliques that have formed gangs to protect themselves against other such gangs in bordering areas. They believe there is a kind of domino effect, fueled by sudden flashes of wide media exposure. Former Bronx District Attorney Burton Roberts, now a judge, believes that the great majority of Bronx street gang members are relatively harmless, and that the major problem is keeping weapons out of their hands and finding them jobs. The present Bronx District Attorney, Mario Merola, took a huge step in this direction by smashing a major gun-running ring in the Bronx in August of 1974.

For obvious reasons of their own, police officials are quick to discount claims by gang leaders that their gangs are helping the neighborhood by running out pushers and junkies and by keeping the block safe. They are probably right in dismissing such claims, though the reason is not simply because all street gangs are engaged in purely antisocial activities. Most of them simply lack the leadership or the motivation to plan and execute long-range projects. Most gang memberships are transitory; members are busted, or move away; they enlist in the Army, or go back to school. A gang may begin with a membership of fifteen to twenty, dominated by two or three more aggressive leaders. By the following summer, only four of the original members, and none of the leaders, may be left, but a whole new crop of members will be sporting the gang's colors. By the following summer, none of the original members may be left; but the gang's name and jackets live on.

Probably fewer than two dozen of the one hundred gangs in the Bronx are serious criminal threats. Thirteen members of the Savage Skulls, for example, were arrested early in 1974 for kidnapping, beating, and raping a couple of thirteen-year-old girls. But the bulk of the gangs sit on concrete stoops outside of crumbling buildings and do nothing for months at a time, hoping each day simply that something exciting will happen, and hoping, too, that if something should really happen, it won't kill them. Most times it doesn't; sometimes, almost by accident, it does.

When the days grew shorter and cooler, the Reapers were left alone on the street. The crowds of little kids that surrounded them, wrestled with them, teased them, to get their attention, were gone. They stood huddled now on the stoop, or against the wall, hiding from the cold. The barriers at the end of the block came down and cars began to line both sides of the street, leaving a barely passable lane between them. The basket came apart again and hung teetering in the wind.

Gang members were thinking about themselves now, of getting some work, maybe, or of joining the Army, or of just getting out of the rut of the street. The gang began to splinter into groups of two and three, and only a few showed up each day to hang out at the basement. Then the super kicked them out of the basement. He was going to fix it up and rent it out, unless, of course, they were willing to pay him some rent. There were a few rumblings about throwing a scare into him, maybe firebombing his apartment, but their hearts weren't in it.

Those that wore their colors wore them as protection against the cooler autumn breezes. By late October, no one bothered to show up in front of the basement any more. Around the neighborhood, huddled against a wall, or in an alleyway, little groups of people could be seen, sharing a joke or a bottle of wine. But Morton Place stayed empty. Exposed to the north, it offered little protection from the Hawkwind that came swooping down in ever-increasing gusts from the river.

Scrawled on the walls of the two corner buildings were the names of some of the more notorious Reapers—Georgie, Eddie, Manny, Luis—painted in faint white letters, in crude graffiti style. The walls were all that reminded passersby of the summers that had passed, and the dirt and the rain and the autumn winds worked hard each day to make that memory fade.

•

October days found Georgie playing pool in a small after-hours club on Tremont Avenue. While the younger Reapers drifted away, thinking of changes they might make in their lives, Georgie sat at a little round table between racks and brooded. Without the Reapers, he was just another broke ex-junkie, looking for a break. He had no job and no money, and his home life was falling apart. Sondra didn't even get angry with him anymore. He went out, she said nothing. He came in, she said nothing. He would ask her if she wanted him to get anything for her while he was out, and she would shake her head. So he said nothing, too.

He stopped brooding when he was finally picked up on violation of probation. He was sent back to Woodburn and spent the three winter months there. He was released on parole again, since it was obvious that drugs were no longer his problem.

When he returned to Harrison Avenue, Sondra was living with another man. He was stunned. He wanted to beg her to let him come back, plead with her to remember the good times together. But he had trouble remembering their good times together. All he could think of was their nonstop fighting, and cool autumn nights lying on a rooftop, dreaming of dope. He wished he had married her; then she wouldn't have found it so damn easy just to kick him out.

He needed a place to stay, and he started moving from place to place, up and down Tremont Avenue, living with friends for a few days at a time. He wanted to stay close to his kids, he told them. He convinced himself that Sondra's new man was a junkie. "I'll kill that motherfucker," he would tell his friends, "if he ever lays a hand on my kids." They would nod gravely; they felt sorry for him. Every week he would scrounge up some bread and buy a present for the children. He would go up to his old house, and Sondra would let him spend a little time with the kids. If the weather was nice, he would take them outside for a short walk. Sondra would meet him at the door and take them back. She didn't ask Georgie to come inside.

He sold his three-cornered sword-cane and his treasured colors. He needed the money desperately. There was no welfare check to get him by anymore, and no big brother to rip off, either. His p.o. really tried this time to get him a job. He sent him down to a few job-training programs, hoping he would sign on for a training course in some basic skill. But Georgie always left when he found out that they didn't pay while they trained. He was twenty-two; he was tired of waiting.

He called up his brother. It was five years since they had spoken to each other, and he took the chance only because he was running out of places to stay. Anyway, he couldn't kill him over the phone. His brother was happy to hear from him, even asked him to come down and crash at his pad for a while. He went down there, rang the bell, and stood there, half ready to run if his brother looked at him cross-eyed. But his brother could afford to be forgiving. He was doing well and enjoyed flaunting it in front of Georgie. He was also genuinely glad that Georgie had managed to kick dope.

He stayed for a week, then left. Twenty years of bad feeling between them didn't disappear overnight, and Georgie began to sense that Eddie was going to start telling him what to do again. He was already bothering him about lounging around the house all day. It was better to go before it all came out again, he thought.

His parole officer set him up for an interview at N.Y.U. They had a program there for school dropouts. They offered courses in paraprofessional careers, like drug counseling or physical therapy for the crippled. Georgie was interested, and the people at N.Y.U. were fascinated with the idea of having an ex-junkie, ex-gang president as a student. He showed up on time for the interview, and everything seemed set. Come back in a week, they told him, and we'll get you registered. But he never showed up again.

They called him at the phone number he had given them. It belonged to a friend whose house he had stayed at for a while. But he wasn't there anymore. The friend said that he hadn't been around for a while. No one knew where he could be, but then it had been a long time since anyone really knew where Georgie was.

He was just gone, back to the rooftops and alleyways, back to the street.